THE REPRODUCTION
OF SOCIAL CONTROL

The Reproduction Of Social Control

A STUDY OF PRISON WORKERS AT SAN QUENTIN

Barbara A. Owen

PRAEGER

New York
Westport, Connecticut
London

Library of Congress Cataloging-in-Publication Data

Owen, Barbara A.
    The reproduction of social control.
    Bibliography: p.
    Includes index.
    1. Correctional personnel—California—San Quentin—
Case studies.   2. California State Prison at San
Quentin—Officials and employees.   I. Title.
HV9475.C3C86   1988   331.7'61365979462   87–36113
ISBN 0–275–92818–7 (alk. paper)

Library of Congress Catalog Card Number: 87–36113
ISBN: 0–275–92818–7

First published in 1988

Praeger Publishers, One Madison Avenue, New York, NY   10010
A division of Greenwood Press, Inc.

Printed in the United States of America

The paper used in this book complies with the
Permanent Paper Standard issued by the National
Information Standards Organization (Z39.48–1984).

10 9 8 7 6 5 4 3 2 1

Contents

Acknowledgments

Many people generously gave help and encouragement to this project. I would like to thank the following individuals and institutions for their support throughout the research and writing of this book. The National Institute of Justice supported this project through their Graduate Fellowship Program. Thanks are due to Anne Schmidt, who helped me in the initial stages of the project. From the University of California at Berkeley, the staff of the Sociology Department and Janice Tanigawa of the Institute for the Study of Social Change gave me administrative support during my field work. David Matza and Troy Duster guided my work in its initial stages. John Irwin aided and abetted my interest in prisons and qualitative methodology. Arlie Hochschild helped with the final production of the book.

In the Bureau of Prisons, several persons should be recognized for their assistance. Lieutenants Jere Cox and Adam Wannamaker made substantive and critical comments on the final draft. Richard Rison, Jerry Alexander, and Helene Cavior deserve mention for their ongoing support. At San Quentin, then-Warden Pulley, Lieutenants Jim McCollough and John Depue, and Mike Madding were instrumental in facilitating my field work. I must add that this book represents my perspective and does not have the official endorsement of the National Institute of Justice, the Bureau of Prisons, the California Department of Corrections, or any of their employees.

I thank Richard Lovick for his special knowledge of prisons and for sharing this experience with me during the course of my fieldwork. His support and encouragement gave me time to write and reflect on the first stages of my analysis. Among my friends and colleagues, Brian Powers offered comments and suggestions from beginning to end. I am particularly grateful to him for our mutual discussions on the idea of social reproduction and for our common vision of sociology. Louise Jezierski and Judy Rothschild helped with the formulation of the project. Barbara Bloom, Terry Arendell, Connie Wisener, Patty Bricker, Matt Leone, and Kathi Keeny also deserve thanks for a variety of reasons.

Many prisoners offered their comments on this work. I am particularly indebted to Tommy and Brian for their help in understanding life in prison. Most importantly, I am grateful to the workers of San Quentin for their willingness to share their world with me. They may not agree with everything said here, but I thank them for the opportunity to view the prison from their perspective. Finally, appreciation is due to George Zimmer and Praeger Publishers for issuing this work.

THE REPRODUCTION
OF SOCIAL CONTROL

1
Introduction: Working in the Pen

Bob Powers is typical of the old-time correctional officers at San Quentin. He is a white, 41-year-old male with prior military experience. After discharge from the army, he worked in a wide variety of manufacturing and service jobs. He eventually applied for positions in local police departments, fire departments, and the California Department of Corrections because he was interested in the job security provided by civil service. He came to work at San Quentin since it was the first to offer him a job. His wife was concerned about the danger of the job, and he admits that he didn't quite know what to expect. But it provided reasonable pay, decent benefits, and job security which he and his family needed.

The period when Bob Powers started work at San Quentin is now called the "good old days." Prior to the late 1970s, most prisons were sheltered from public inquiry and shielded by a hands-off policy endorsed by the courts. The warden of the "Big House" (Irwin, 1980) enjoyed almost absolute power over his prisoners and his workers. Prisoners' rights—soon to become an issue in the turbulent years to follow—were treated subjectively by the staff. The warden and his staff set the tone for the definition and treatment of prisoners. When Bob Powers came on the job in the early 1970s, the prison population was high and the number of officers was low. Most officers were similar to him in background and demographics—white men with military backgrounds. Like other new officers,

Bob Powers received little training for his new job. He described his idea of the job as,

> guarding prisoners . . . well I thought that I would have a gun, or a set of handcuffs on an inmate—he was the bad guy and I was the good guy. But then they told me that I wouldn't have a gun on the ground and to always watch my back—and I still do that. That was about it for my training. But then once you get inside those walls, you find out it's a lot more than that.

As he became familiar with the world of the prison, Bob Powers learned the contours of prison culture and developed a personal strategy for dealing with prisoners. He found that interaction with prisoners was a key to the job and "talking to them and really listening" was the best way to get the job done.

During the 1970s, the prison was changing in many ways. Along with the increased racial/ethnic consciousness of the prisoners, the society outside the walls was beginning to respond to entrenched inequalities of race and sex. Affirmative action goals were set by the state and the prison made an active effort to hire minority and later, female workers in male institutions. As prisoners began to assert their claim to legal rights (Fogel, 1979), the courts began to grant them greater legal protection. Prison workers also began to organize duing this period, becoming unionized as well as working for the professionalization of their jobs. These changes, along with shifting images of prisoners and the introduction of minorities and women into the prison labor force (Jacobs and Retsky, 1975), have significantly altered the occupational culture of "working in the pen."

George Elliot was one of the first black men to join the correctional staff at the prison. His story illustrates many aspects of contemporary worker culture. He has a military background and several years of college preparation in law enforcement. A college friend who was on the staff encouraged him to apply for a job at San Quentin. For George Elliot, this was a step toward a career as a police officer on the street. Feeling that he was too young to hit the streets, he thought that the prison would make him ready for that job, which he saw as more demanding. But working at San Quentin entailed a number of problems for the young 23-year-old correctional officer. Among these problems was the existence of a ruling clique of officers and administrators who ran the prison. Most of these officers were white and George Elliot was very conscious of his minority status:

When I first came here there were only a few black officers. When you would see one you would give a little smile and say, oh good, there is another one. When I first started working here, I worked a lot of positions where it was just me and the rest of them were white . . . just little old me out there. It was good when there was another black working because then you can go stand by them and you don't look so funny standing there by yourself. Now I know almost all the officers and it's different, but back then you were just looking for a friend, someone you could turn to and not worry that they would say something about you as soon as you looked the other way.

Along with Bob Powers, George Elliot also believes that talking to prisoners is the most successful style of working in the pen. "We talk about everything—girls, sports, the streets." Another area of agreement between Powers and Elliot is a shared attitude toward women. Both have an ambivalent perspective on female officers in a male, maximum security prison. Elliot explains:

In a way it is good and in a way it is not. The bottom line for me is that this is no place for a woman to work. I believe in equal opportunity, but there are positions that women should not work. There are big guys in here—she may be able to run fast and get help, but if it came down to a brawl, and heads were busted, it is no place for a woman. There are so many women now—I think it keeps the place calmed down. I don't think this is the place for a woman but it has worked out . . . if nothing is happening the women can do the job.

One of the women who "can do the job" is Kathy Peters. She is white and has a bachelor's degree in social science. At 26, starting work at San Quentin was a considered choice, a challenge to her social ideals. When she came to work at the end of the 1970s, the open violence of the earlier decade had been replaced by a more stable order due to the tightening of security. Racial conflict among the prisoners remained a basis for social organization, but racism had become less of a problem among the officers. Sexism and a resistance to female officers, however, continued to divide the staff. Peters is seen by some male workers as a good officer because she "works like a man" and "isn't afraid of popping them [prisoners] in the mouth if they deserve it." This is in contrast to opinions on other women who "act too macho" and "seem to forget that they are women when they walk through the gate."

Bob Powers, George Elliot, and Kathy Peters represent three significant elements of correctional officer culture. Their careers illustrate shifts in both the structure and culture of the prison and the implications these changes have for the worker culture. This study focuses on two basic relationships in correctional officer culture: relations with prisoners and relations with coworkers. This emphasis leads to the investigation of a broader issue in prison studies—the reproduction of social control in the prison.

The prison has long occupied a central role in the study of social control. These studies, however, have been limited to describing the nature of the *prisoner* culture, ignoring the role of the prison worker in the production and maintenance of social control in the prison. As Melossi (1985) has recently suggested, the "motivational constructs employed by agents of social control" require investigation. This study is concerned with these social accounts—the way prison workers come to define their role in the prison, and, in doing so, become an agent of the institutional mechanisms of social control. The study of the worldview of the worker and its role in the reproduction of social control blends two separate approaches to the study of the prison. One approach has been a concentration on a structural analysis of the prison (Haynor and Ash, 1939; McKorkle and Korn, 1954; Sykes and Messinger, 1960; Garabedian, 1963; Thomas and Petersen, 1977; Duffee, 1975; Sykes, 1956; McCleary, 1960; Jacobs, 1979; Wright, 1973; and Cloward *et al.*, 1960). Microsociological descriptions of prison culture constitute a second approach to the study of social control (Clemmer, 1940; Schragg, 1944; Irwin and Cressey, 1962; Irwin, 1970; Manocchio and Dunn, 1970; Cressey, 1960; Irwin, 1980; Carroll, 1977 and 1974; Jacobs, 1974; Davidson, 1974; Burns, 1969; Jacobs, 1977; Weinberg, 1942; and Sykes, 1956). These two approaches have left a gap in understanding the prison as an active, living institution of social control. A description of the activity by which social control is translated from the interactional level to the structural level is needed to elaborate the connection between the culture and the structure of the prison. A description is needed of the ways in which social control is both produced and distributed differentially throughout the prison community. This study also examines social order and the ways in which it is produced and maintained through the actions of its members.

In the prison, social control affects the workers themselves. As employees, the worker is also subjected to the very forces which he or she is, on the surface, charged with introducing onto the prisoner. Social control is a product of relations among human beings, acting and reacting within the institutional context of the prison. This context is shaped by power and the expression of interests specific to the prison community. These interests flow from the prison administration and the central administration of the state and may not be identical to the interests of the line worker in the prison.

The reciprocity of social control is the key to understanding its reproduction. This study suggests that the worker is both a subject and an object of social control within the dynamics of the prison social order. As the worker subjects the prisoner to the demands of social control he or she is also subjected to the very same demands for rule-governed behavior. In the prison, these rules are both formal, as articulated in the laws and administrative codes, and informal, as power and interests are negotiated through interaction. The paramilitary organization of the prison formal social structure, the high levels of competition among workers, and the traditions of racism and sexism in the prison create a subtle, yet complicated, web of social control for the worker as well.

Like other concepts which explain life in prison, such as prison culture and the deprivations of imprisonment, description and analysis of the worker meaningworld illuminates the very structure of the prison itself. As conveyed by the concept of "structuration" (Giddens, 1979) and the "self-production of society" (Touraine, 1977), this inquiry assumes that social structure is, in fact, a process which exists only through the actions and interactions of its participants. Examination of these actions and their attendant meanings also reveals the very nature of the institutional structure. Touraine makes this point well:

Human society possesses a capacity of symbolic creation by the means of which, between a situation and social conduct, there occurs the formation of meaning, a system of orientation of conduct. Human society is the only natural system known to possess this capacity to form and transform its functioning on the basis of its investments and the image it has of its capacity to act on itself (Touraine, 1977, p. 4).

The development of meaningworlds reflects the ongoing, lived experience of the worker. Social control, like other institutional forms, is a skilled performance of social beings. These skills are obtained through direct contacts with other actors whose behavior reflect relations of power and interests. Giddens (1979) argues that social practice is embedded in language. Through a process of symbolic interaction, individuals interpret these offered meanings and tailor them to their own subjective interests. This book describes this reproductive process.

Studying social control is not a simple task. As E. P. Thompson says about the difficulty of studying another sociological construct, "class":

Like any other relationship, it is a fluency which evades analysis if we attempt to stop it dead at any given moment and atomize its structure. The finest-meshed sociological net cannot give us a pure specimen of class, any more than it can give us one of deference or of love. The relationship must always be embodied in real people in a real context (Thompson, 1963, p. 9).

Toward this end, this study examines the reproduction of social control as it exists in the meanings, actions, and relationships of those charged with custody and security in the prison.

THE LOCATION OF THIS INVESTIGATION: SAN QUENTIN

Among institutions of social control, San Quentin stands as a symbol of severest punishment. Inside these walls are prisoners judged to be the most dangerous to society. As part of a large state prison system, San Quentin receives California's maximum custody prisoners. San Quentin is also a place of work for several hundred employees. During the course of the workday, the prison worker interacts with all members of the prison community. This interaction and the corresponding relationships shape the social organization of the prison. Relations with prisoners illustrate the translation—and the transmutations—of social control in the prison. Relations with workers reveal the ways in which these forces of social control act upon the workers themselves. The following chapters describe these relations which sustain the reproduction of social control.

San Quentin State Prison is a maximum security prison on the San Francisco Bay. Traditionally this prison held prisoners convicted of serious felonies. The prison has the walls, towers, and physical dimensions of the "Big House" as described by Irwin (1980). The physical dimensions of the prison are marked by five-tiered cell blocks, the "Big Yard," the walls that surround the entire housing area, and gun towers which guard the perimeter of the prison.

Until the early 1980s, prisoners of most classifications had some amount of movement inside the prison. For those who were able to "program," jobs, school, and vocational training allowed movement during the daylight hours. Other activities, such as visits, meals, appointments, errands, and "hustles" also contributed to a constant flow of prisoners throughout the prison. Due to changes in policy and the escalation of violence within the institution, these activities have been severely modified. Movement within the institution and the availability of programs appear to have decreased as the social order of the prison shifts toward a more restrictive order.

Prison social order is shaped by the nature of its population and the policies of the administration. At the time of this research, the population was a somewhat heterogenous mix of custody levels. Once a prisoner was assigned to San Quentin, his routine within the institution was determined primarily by this custody level. In the honor block, for example, the levels of privileges were only limited by the walls of the institution. Prisoners who lived here had access to their own canteen, exercise yard, and ordinarily did not have to "lock up" (return to their cells) until 10 P.M.. The majority of prisoners with custodies between medium and maximum are designated "general population" or mainline. Prisoners requiring the greatest security and those sentenced to death are housed in separate units. For example, at the time of this research, the North Block housed maximum security prisoners and segregated these prisoners according to gang affiliation (with corresponding tiers for those designated "nonaffiliated"). Movement in North Block was severely restricted and under escort by a correctional worker. These prisoners are likely to spend the most time in "lock down." Death row was also a separate unit. Prisoners here await determination of their death penalty sentences and live in a self-contained unit. The Adjustment Center (AC) held the prisoners deemed disciplinary problems. Irwin (1980, p. 203) suggests that such custody designations are systems of "hierarchical segregation that encourage withdrawal and conformity and greatly reduce contact between prisoners. As such, prison architecture itself functions to produce and maintain social control."

These living units and their levels of privilege undergo constant change. During the fieldwork, the honor block lost its level of privileges and mobility and was converted to a "workers' " block for prisoners whose labor maintains the institution. Much of the South Block and East Block, which formerly housed mainline prisoners, had been converted into lock up units, much like the North Block. These changes altered the day-to-day activities of the prison community and changed the stability of the prison social order. Previously, San Quentin was seen by many convicts and workers as "the best place to do time." Although confined to a life inside the walls, the availability of activities and programs provided some semblance of a productive life among the prisoners. Since many prisoners had lived continuously at San Quentin for years, and many expected to remain there, a prisoner social system developed that was somewhat stable and predictable. Prisoners who amassed "juice" (that is, influence and power) developed a vested interest in the existing social order and exerted their influence over other prisoners to not rock the boat. At San Quentin, it appears that the prisoner population is becoming much younger, more violent (in terms of criminal and institutional histories), and less involved in the activities which contribute to the stable social order of the prison. In some respects, the rise of the gangs—and the corresponding fear of this rise—has also shaped the prison social order (Irwin, 1980; Porter, 1982).

These recent changes must be understood against an historical context. Two representative studies of the history of San Quentin and the California prison system are Lamott (1961) and Yaley and Platt (1982). The most definitive history of San Quentin itself is found in *Chronicles of San Quentin* (Lamott, 1961). In providing details of the day-to-day activities in the nascent California prison, Lamott gives insight into the development of the themes and traditions that shaped this contemporary prison.

Lamott's work is also important in that he provides concrete information on the development of the work force. The initial workers at San Quentin were recruited from wherever they could be found. The first prison director was ambivalent about his new work force, noting that they were "brave and desperate men, but somewhat addicted to dissipation" (Lamott, 1961, p. 25). This dissipation included drinking and consorting with the female prisoners. Alcohol was not only readily available to the new workers, but also available to certain prisoners. Lamott notes that the

democracy of drinking . . . blurred even the line between the guards and the convicts. In fact, many visitors complained they could not tell the difference between the two. Both guards and prisoners wore shabby clothes and appeared to be drunk. Some prisoners even carried guns. The problem of alcohol among the workers continued, causing some writers at the time to claim that the guard line at Point Quentin was a refuge for reformed alcoholics (Lamott, 1961, p. 26).

The low pay, the long hours (originally 18 hours, seven days a week), and the dangerous conditions did not attract a competent work force. Escapes were commonplace and many workers were killed or maimed "whilst in the discharge of their duty" (Lamott, 1961, p. 25).

Yaley and Platt (1982) illustrate the historical development of social control in the prison within a political-economic context. The following chronology is taken from their work on the dynamics of the developing California prison system. In 1851, the California legislature contracted with General Vallejo and his partner, Major Estell, to "provide for the security of the state prison convicts" (Yaley and Platt, 1982, p. 72). Previously, felons were incarcerated in old Mexican jails and barges scattered around the state. In December 1851, the barge *Euphemia* was floated on San Francisco Bay to be used as a prison ship. The conditions on the *Euphemia* were said to be horrible; the ship was a "private hell hole" with air so foul that "only the most seasoned and resolute guards were able to descend into the ship to unlock the convicts" (Brown, quoted in Yaley and Platt, 1982, p. 78). On other prison ships, such as the *Wabu*, guards refused to go below until the ship was aired out.

On July 7, 1852, land at Point San Quentin was purchased for the new prison. By 1854, the first cell block was erected, using convict labor. In 1859, the "Dungeon" and the women's prison was built. This structure is now used for the prison hospital as women were moved to a new facility at Tehachepi in 1932. Upon completion of this construction, a committee formed by the California legislature found that the new prison was "no paradise for scoundrels," it was a "real penitentiary—a place of suffering and expiation" (quoted in Yaley and Platt, 1982, p. 87). Yaley and

Platt suggest that mismanagement and corruption plagued the private administration of the prison. Prisoners were ill-clothed and inadequately fed. In 1855, the state began to assert control over the prison and by 1858 the state assumed total control. Inedible food, harsh discipline, and inhumane conditions characterized the prison. Escapes were common and brought unwanted attention. By 1864, the state increased the number of guards in response to citizen complaints. To induce compliant behavior and a willingness to work, an incentive system of "good time" credits was also introduced at that time.

In the 1930s, the inhumane prison conditions received public attention. Brutality by the guards and the unrest of the prisoners were investigated by the state authorities. In 1938, Governor Olson conducted an investigation of the brutal conditions, which established new policies concerning physical brutality. Despite this intervention, physical punishment continued to shape social control in California's prisons. In the early 1940s, California began to search for new forms of social control to handle its prison populations. Yee (1973) describes this shift toward rehabilitative ideal and its effect on California prisons.

In the 1940s and 1950s, the revival of the rehabilitative ideal introduced the concept of pathology to definitions of the prisoner. This image supported a clinical model of "corrections" and implied the notions of sickness and treatment. This treatment was to be delivered by a new wave of workers, most importantly the "correctional officer" and a staff of counselors and psychologists. A wide range of treatment strategies were developed within this context of the "rehabilitative ideal" as the new institutional response. Dissatisfaction with rehabilitation (American Friends Service Committee, 1971; Fogel, 1979) led California to reconsider its mode of social control. In 1977, California returned to a determinate sentence model and abandoned much of the rehabilitative model. Despite the movement toward punishment or "just dessert" models, many institutions continue to use the language of the correctional model in describing this world. Correctional officer is now the standard term used for the prison worker.

This very brief chronology illustrates some of the history of California prisons and provides a context for understanding the role of the prison worker. From the early days of the turnkey to the prison guard to the modern correctional worker, the role of the worker is embedded in the operation of social control. This study argues that social control in the prison is rooted in interaction, both between workers and prisoners and among the work force itself. This interaction in turn is mediated by several factors which tie together meaning and action and shape the world-view of the worker. Chapter 2 details the elements that shape the meaningworld of the worker. The conflicts and contradictions of the social structure of the prison are primary elements of this construction. Chapter 3 describes the variety of possible relationships among workers and prisoners. Common interests, such as keeping the peace, avoiding violence, and getting through the day illustrate these intersections. Antagonistic relations are also discussed. Chapter 4 concerns relations among the workers themselves. Here, conflicts of interests and clashing images of prisoners divide the work force. Race and gender, years of service, and career orientations shape these relations. Chapter 5 reviews previous descriptions of the worker role and suggests a new typology which is grounded in the reproduction of social control. This typology reflects levels of reconciliation of the conflicts and contradictions that shape the worker's world. Chapter 6 articulates the central elements of power, interests, meaning, and interaction. A review of the literature is contained in the Appendix.

2
Elements of the Worldview

In this analysis, the worldview of the worker is a crucial element in the reproduction of social control. The worldview of the worker reflects and re-creates dimensions of the prison culture and corresponding social structure. This social structure can be revealed through the actions of its members and illustrates the basis of prison social order. Here the term "social structure" refers to an ongoing, dynamic social process which structures action in a given collectivity. Giddens's (1979) work on the duality of structures and the notion of structuration notes the essential recursiveness of social life as it is constituted in social practice. This connection is made through the meaningworld of the actor and is produced and reproduced through social practices. Language and relationships with other actors are examples of such social practice.

As an agent of social control, the worker is the point at which the power and the coercion of the prison is delivered. As social actors, the worker occupies a reflexive role in the structure of the prison. Therefore, the worker develops a system of meanings and relations that approximates the contours of this world. As each worker becomes socialized into the prison community, he or she learns the culture of social control and its surrounding meaning-systems. These meanings and relations are derived from interaction on the shop floor of the prison with workers, administrators, and prisoners. Through this interaction a worker develops a worldview which serves as the motive force of his or her actions.

CONFLICTS AND CONTRADICTIONS

The perspective of the prison worker reflects the structural and personal conflicts of the job and the prison itself. Each of these conflicts and contradictions presents ambiguous meanings about the prison to the worker. In attempting to make sense of this world, each worker must reconcile these contradictions in a way that allows the worker to get through the workday. The development of these personal perspectives may also contribute to the alienation of the worker. Through experience, workers come to define the job in their own terms because a consistent perspective on the job is not obtainable from the worker subculture. Toch and Klofas (1982) discuss this process in terms of a "pluralistic ignorance" and suggest that the individualized worldviews prohibit workers from developing a unified definition of the situation. The components that shape these conflicts are discussed below.

Structural and Institutional Conflict

The structural conflicts and contradictions of the prison are well documented (Wright, 1973; Cressey, 1959; Irwin, 1980). The clash between rehabilitation and custody, the struggle for scarce fiscal resources with other agencies of the state, and the conflicts between the central administration and the individual prisons create a structure in which these conflicts are manifested. As an institution of social control, and one charged with conflicting functions (for example, custody and rehabilitation), the members of the prison community must develop a meaningsystem which mediates these contradictions.

Cressey (1959) has argued that the contradictory directives of the modern prison contribute to the structural problems. In focusing on the conflict between the demands of custody and the demands of rehabilitation, Cressey and others (Irwin, 1980; American Friends Service Committee, 1971) suggest that prisons are fundamentally contradictory institutions. Cressey notes, as an example, the problems inherent in rule enforcement. In a formal sense, the rules and regulations are codified in written form. But every experienced worker knows, and new workers soon discover, that the rule book does not cover all situations of working in the pen. These rules must be applied subjectively: a solution may not be found in the formal definition of the situation. As an illustration, Cressey cites a speech given to new workers:

You are here to enforce the rules of the institution. Every rule. If we thought that one of these rules was not needed, we would throw them out . . . so don't ever fail to enforce a rule even if you think it is nonsense. It is there for a reason. Don't blow hot and cold. Enforce the same rule in the same way everyday. Come and see me if you think a rule does not make sense. We will take it up. But if it is there, enforce it (quoted in Cressey, 1959, p. 481).

The administration's attempt to retain control over the rule-enforcement process is one of the ways the worker is subjected to the general social control operating in the prison. The lack of worker authority and autonomy is also noted by Cressey (1959, p. 482). But the worker responds to these attempts at social control in practical ways. In response to the prohibitions against talking to prisoners, an experienced worker remarks, "I talk to them all the time. How in the hell are you going to get anything done if you do not talk to them . . . to hell with them [the administration], just keep talking to them" (Cressey, 1959, p. 485).

The hierarchy and paramilitary organization of the prison give rise to intense power struggles that affect the administration, the line staff, and the prisoners. At the top of this hierarchy, the warden and his administration seek to maintain existing power relations through a number of official and informal ways. As the state prison system becomes more consolidated under the authority in the state capital, individual prisons are losing their former autonomy. Until very recently, the state prison system operated somewhat independently of the state corrections system and other institutions. Each prison was viewed as an individual "fiefdom" and was generally exempt from outside scrutiny. This process has occurred in the last several decades. Jacobs (1977) and Yee (1973) describe the ways in which the prison became less of a closed institution and more subject to public and court scrutiny. However, the existence of judicial review, the politicization of prisoners and other elements of social change served to highlight the power struggles of the prison. Control over staff and prisoners is central to these struggles.

The struggle for institutional power shapes formal and informal relationships. The pursuit of power—known in the prison as "juice,"—characterizes the formal hierarchy and often shapes personal relationships among staff and administration. "Being in the car," that is, having a definite, but informal, personal relationship with those in power, becomes the goal of those who aspire to personal power in the institution. Formal relationships with the power structure take the shape of promotions and occupation of certain positions in the paramilitary order. Upward mobility, however, is not only limited to official position. Having "juice," and "being in the car," can also be a result of clique membership. (The term "clique" is also used to describe the prisoner network, see Irwin, 1980.) The ruling cliques in the prison have access to the power structure in informal ways. Such relationships as "dads and kids" illustrate an individualized access to the power structure. In return for such opportunities, informal power seekers must contribute to the maintenance of the established order through their behavior and definitions of the situation. Often, these informal relationships with power and the personal investment in the status quo lead to formal rewards such as promotions, but also to informal rewards such as status, juice, and desired positions. Competition for these personalized relationships further contributes to the personal struggles described below.

Personal Conflicts

The personal and individualized conflicts of the job are related directly to the structural conflict described above. The contradictory goals and function of the prison, the struggle for power and the divergence between action and experience all translate into conflicts and contradictions in the day-to-day routine of the correctional worker. The restricted access to upward mobility and the discretionary distribution of informal power contribute to competition among the workers in a fundamental way. This competition is modified somewhat by the location of interests by each worker.

These interests are further informed by the motivations for entering the field of corrections, for staying on the job, and for leaving. Definitions and interests on the shop floor of the prison are related to one's motivations for doing the job. Those who enter the job with a professional career orientation are most likely to pursue the formal avenues of power, and to perform the job "by the book." Those who define their work as only a job may locate their interests around such issues as getting through the day, avoiding hassles and violence, and keeping things cool. Others may personalize their job and develop interests that connect their area of responsibility (for example, the tier or work unit) to some personal pride. Still others come to the job with a humanitarian orientation and may build their interests around helping or rehabilitation. Whatever the evolution of interests, these interests are directly tied to a specific version of the world, attendant to definitions and meanings which inform behavior and attitudes as well as tied to a particular relationship with those in the legitimate power structure. This combination of definitions, interests, and power relations becomes the cornerstone for the development of the worldview of the correctional worker.

Because the worldview evolves through interaction, it is a dynamic process. As the worker gains experience and interacts with the wide range of situations and individuals who make up the prison community, these motivations, definitions, and interests may change. For example, the worker who enters with a career orientation may discover that chances for promotions are unlikely and may shift orientations toward other interests. Discovering the stress and tension associated with the work may deter those who enter the job as a challenge. Additionally, the shape of the relationship to power may change over time—as administrations shift or as one's mentor (a relationship known as "dads and kids") transfers or promotes. The dynamic nature of interests, meanings, and power relationships creates a worldview grounded in unstable elements and susceptible to covert and subtle levels of competition among the workers.

These conflicts in definitions and behavior often aggravate the difficult nature of the job itself. The meaningworld and perspective of the corrections worker are constructed through the reconciliation of these conflicts. As institutional struggles for power can affect line staff, a second level of struggle shapes the relationships at work. The stages in the development of the worldview correspond directly to the resolution of these conflicts. As each worker becomes more submerged in these conflicts, their attempts to solve them occur in patterned and systematic ways. This pattern is the world-view of the correctional worker and has a wide range of consequences for the prison as a whole. Shifting definitions and shifting allegiances contribute to the unstable nature of the prison social order. The consequences arising from this instability include violence, a high turnover rate, incompetent job performance, and measures of alienation (for example, suicide, substance abuse, and divorce).

This image of the correctional worker is significantly different from that suggested in previous research. The root of its misperception lies in an inaccurate statement of the job and has relied on the official definitions of the job. In order to construct a more accurate image of the correctional worker, the limits of the job, its interaction and contradictions must be fully described.

CONCEPTUAL THEMES: MEANING, POWER, AND INTERACTION

For the prison worker, reconciliation of both structural and personal conflicts is based on three conceptual themes: meaning, power, and interaction. These concepts are central to the reproduction of social control.

Meaning

The construction of meaning plays a significant role in the reproduction of social control. Meaning systems allow an actor to act
intentionally, to form a response to the behavior of others and
shape the construction of a worldview that informs behavior. Prison
culture is a curious hybrid of meanings. Operating as a world unto
its own, yet composed of actors who bring to bear their experience
from the outside world, prison culture combines elements of the
inside and the outside worlds. Within this normative system, everyday pleasures, such as privacy, autonomy, and mobility are ex-
pressly forbidden, common commodities become contraband, and
small acts of rudeness or imagined insults escalate into major acts
of violence. Seemingly innocuous objects, such as a toothbrush,
can be turned into a deadly weapon. A tube of shampoo can be
transformed into a syringe for injecting drugs. The racial prejudice
of the outside world is transformed into open segregation and hostilities. At the same time, demands are made that bring out the
strength of the human spirit. Simple acts of kindness, unnoticed
on the streets, become monuments to this same spirit. To the
uninitiated, both worker and prisoner, this normative system appears chaotic and senseless. Indeed, the social order of the prison
and its attendant meaningworlds are negotiated and fragile. Un-
derneath the surface, systems of meanings structure relations in
the prison and thus shape prison culture. Fundamental to this social
order are the deprivations of imprisonment (Sykes, 1958) and the
forces of outside society (Irwin and Cressey, 1962). The prison is
not strictly isolated from the general culture, but instead writes a
unique version of society on its members. Meanings in the prison
must be understood as a reflection of the social structure of the
prison itself.

Power

Very simply, prisons are fundamentally involved with the creation and use of power. Power and its reproduction thus frame this

investigation of the prison and its workers. On a structural level, the prison embodies the power of social control, and a monopoly over violence and coercion, as granted by the state. Within the institution, power is distributed both formally and informally. The warden and staff are charged with the administration of this power bestowed by the state. Acting within the formal framework defined by law and administrative decree, this formal power outwardly shapes social control within the prison. Informally, a network of prisoners, workers, and administrators operate within the context of practical power, or "juice" in the prison argot. Those with juice can go beyond the formal delineation of roles and rules, wielding a type of power that transcends institutional boundaries.

The formal structure of the prison provides for a systematic distribution of power through the ranks. The warden and the administration occupy the top of the hierarchy, and like the military, other specific authority is passed down through assistant administrators, captains, lieutenants, sergeants, and finally to the line officer. For those occupying formal positions of power, maintaining and increasing their power base becomes a preoccupation. Making the right allegiances, developing juice through personalized relationships, and extending one's turf and upward mobility are key activities associated with these roles. At the upper levels of the hierarchy, concerns with prisoners are secondary to concerns over maintaining the status quo. In a series of articles in the *Sacramento Bee*, Wilson (1981) describes the benefits of "being in the car" with George Sumner, the previous warden. Other articles in this series describe corruption and power moves on the part of the staff. One statement from these articles was also echoed throughout this investigation. "It wasn't the inmates. I could handle the inmates. And it was not the stress of being in a hostile environment. It was the shit we had to take from [Sumner and Larson]. . . . "

For the correctional worker, these relationships become a defining facet of their employment. Access to such relationships is limited and distributes competition among workers in significant ways. However, not all workers see obtaining this power as a goal or motivation. These workers may opt out of the competition, through seeking nondesirable jobs and watch assignments or developing an individual niche that is not in direct competition with the power seekers. Evidence suggests that this course is one taken by many officers who remain in the employment of the California Department of Corrections. Unless one makes progress both up the career ladder and in the informal power network, one comes to recognize the futility of their endeavor. The dynamics of power in the prison direct the inquiry into the reproduction of social control. As such, the worker's relationship to institutional and informal operations of power is a direct influence in the construction of the worldview.

Interests

The interests of actors are corollary to both power and meaning. Members of the prison community act intentionally, in ways that appear, subjectively, to serve self-interest. In discussing this idea of self-interest Burawoy (1979, p. 19) suggests that struggles on the shop floor are struggles over the realization of interests. The conflicts and contradictions of the prison find expression in these competing interests of prisoners, workers and administrators. At first glance, the interests of workers and prisoners may appear to be antagonistic. The tenets of the prison code (Sykes and Messinger, 1960) suggest that these interests of workers and prisoners are mutually exclusive. In this view, the interests of the worker and the administration would be quite similar. However, a close examination of the routine of the worker finds little evidence of this assumed relationship. In the everyday life of the tier, the worker and the prisoner confront common, overlapping interests. Such interests generally relate to common goals, such as keeping the peace, avoiding violence, and a smooth operation of the daily routine (meals, visits, exercise, etc.). Violence, a disrupted routine, or a total lock down do not serve the general interests of the prison community. Such disruptions however, may serve specific self-interests, such as diverting the attention of "the man" for purposes of an assault. Worker and prisoner interest coincide on several dimensions. The peaceful tier, the smooth-running job as-signment, and the absence of tension are common goals for prisoner and worker and are shared, if implicit, interests.

The crucial aspect of this interaction lies in the potential for developing a mutual set of interests for the worker and the prisoners. The desire to get through the day, accomplish the tasks at hand (mail delivery, meals, visits, training, work assignments, and the like) and avoid confrontation, hassle, and violence are shared interests of worker and prisoner. Through interaction and conversation, each comes to recognize these mutual interests in an individualized way. This process does not uniformly occur, but instead becomes individualized and situational. In Chapter 3, the origin and the substance of these relations will be described. These relationships and the subsequent recognition of mutual interest occur only through individual interaction.

The conflicts of interests among the workers are also of concern. The competition for the scarce rewards of working in the pen, the conflicts over definitions of the job and working styles may divide the workers among themselves. Some research suggests that prison staff do not understand their coworkers' perspectives (Toch and Klofas, 1982; Duffee, 1979). Combined with the high levels of competition among the workers, this likelihood of communication and of sharing positive definitions about prisoners is diminished.

The particularized nature of the interaction between worker and prisoner, the high levels of competition among workers for scarce resources, and the separating effects of the prison ideology create barriers for coworker interactions that are very difficult to surmount. Thus, the correctional worker is faced with a dilemma of perspectives. The version of the world offered by the administration is grounded in the maintenance of power relations whereas the lived-through experience of the worker suggests a set of interests that are antagonistic to these relations. The contradiction shaped by these conflicts determines the worker's approach to the job, the meanings subscribed to workers and prisoners, and the shape of conceptions of self and others. These contradictions and their resolutions engineer the worldview of the correctional worker.

The contemporary occupational structure of prison work casts the line worker and the administration into adversarial roles. The rise of collective bargaining, the need for "cost-effective" management, and conflicts in definitions of the job shape these conflicts (Jacobs and Crotty, 1978, 1981). Like work relations on the street, there is significant conflict between management and staff in the correctional world. As staff unite over issues such as safety, prison conditions, and increased wages and benefits, prison administrators are forced into a traditional management policy in negotiating these demands downward.

Another conflict of interest between worker and administration comes through a difference in perspectives on the job itself. In meeting the demands of the job, the prison staff develop a set of meanings grounded in the day-to-day experience of the shop floor. The perspective of the administration, in contrast, is grounded in bureaucratic demands and is essentially removed from the demands of interaction on the tier. With few exceptions, administrators (and many superior officers) have little face-to-face contact with prisoners. Many have reached their positions in the modern prison through education or political appointment, rather than up through the ranks (Jacobs, 1977). This difference of perspective, as grounded in interaction, meanings, and interests contributes to a fundamental conflict in ideology between the line staff and the administration.

Interaction

Descriptions of the prison social order from Clemmer (1940) through Irwin (1980) agree on one primary fact: Prison social order is grounded in social relationships among members of the prison community. These relationships may be antagonistic, as with the "tips and cliques" described by Irwin (1980), materially based, as described by Williams and Fish (1974), or symbiotic as the relationship between the keepers and the kept described by Sykes (1958). Prison research has found consistently that social relationships are the fundamental basis from the prison social order.

The interruption of these relationships contributes to rapid social change in the prison social structure.

Relationships of mutual interest between the keeper and the kept are the basis for the informal social order in the prison. In the development of an approach to the job, the new recruit may not recognize the crucial nature of these common interests or relationships. New recruits are not equipped with a set of meanings that allow them to immediately "make sense" of the prison. From this inexperience, the fundamental basis of the prison social order is obscured in the mind of the new worker. As the worker gains experience and develops the "common sense" so critical to working in the prison, a contradiction in these definitions takes shape in the emerging worldview of the correctional worker. The resolution of this contradiction is the basis for the worldview of the correctional officer. The nature and content of interaction with prisoners, workers, and the administration shapes the nature of the confrontation and its ultimate resolution.

The conceptual themes of meaning, power, and interaction provide the framework for analyzing the problematic nature of social control. As the institutional contradictions emerge in the role of the worker, gaps in meaning and power shape the perspectives of the worker. The resolution of these conflicts contributes to the worldview of the worker and the negotiation of social control.

3
Intersections of Interests: Relations with Prisoners

Interaction and face-to-face relations with prisoners are primary socialization experiences for all correctional workers. These contacts are mediated by a range of factors that shape the meaning and definitions of these encounters. Interaction with prisoners is both fundamental and problematic to the construction of the world of the worker. One step in this construction is the recognition of common interests among workers and prisoners.

INITIAL CONTACT

Initial contacts with prisoners are problematic for the new employee. For most workers, exposure to prisons has been minimal, although they appear to be curious about the prisoners. Few workers are familiar with the justice system and are relatively unfamiliar with the process that leads to incarceration. New workers (and new prisoners) are referred to by the term "fish." The first appearance of fish workers marks the symbolic reception of newcomers into the prison community. In *Grimhaven* (Trasker, 1927), an early account of prison life at San Quentin, the reception given to new workers is described:

The new guards—the fish bulls—were shoving and poking men about in the line. They bawled foolish things instead of giving quiet commands. The horde of prisoners are malleable, even as any other group of men, if the commands are intelligently given. But confused, bellowed orders breed turmoil. Guards, in particular the green, country louts, were booed as they floundered self-consciously along the lines, striving to bring about discipline. Occasionally a particularly hotheaded guard would attempt to capture the culprits who booed him and made vulgar noises with his mouth for his discomfiture. And then! The discipline was a burlesque. Laughter and jeers were in the air. An ugly overtone of excitement and hatred spread throughout the prison (Tasker, 1927, pp. 124–25).

The "boos and vulgar noises" described above continue to greet the new correctional worker. The first exposure to prisoners most likely comes during the initial tours of the prison. Prisoners will generally line up along the tier railings in the cell blocks, or at some distance from the touring new workers. The prisoners will reach into their arsenal of insults and shout comments peculiar to the culture of the prison, as well as general remarks about one's appearance, masculinity, and abilities. For the worker who reacts to these taunts, a new set of remarks are projected that detail this reaction. For male workers, the challenge to one's masculinity is always present. Women seem to deal with these insults with less reaction, perhaps due to the socialization against taunts in the outside world. In a novelized version of the prisoners' experience, Brady (1967) describes the treatment of a new male worker, Preston, during his first appearance in the tier:

Then Preston heard a sound he dreaded. In one of the cells just across from him an inmate hidden in the darkness was pushing air through his teeth to make a noise like air leaking from a punctured inner tube, bubbling through the spit. Preston knew what to expect.

"See the sweet little bull?" an anonymous voice asked in a tone that conveyed both amusement and obscenity.

Preston jerked his eyes away. He felt his face grow hot. Pay no attention to them, his watch lieutenant had told him: If they see they're getting to you, they'll never let go.

"Pussy on the gun rail," another voice called.

"Hey sucker, don't rank my action," the first voice continued with mock seriousness, "I saw her first. Didn't I baby? Slip over here to the tier and I will give it to you through the bars" (Brady, 1967, p. 52).

The first exposure is a rite of passage for the new workers. Such events test the mettle of the new worker and gauge their responses. Prisoners are searching for clues as to how they may "get over" while other workers and superior officers are looking for defects or "weaknesses." In the prison, strength, weakness, and the all important respect are the cornerstones of social order. For the worker who depends on anticipating the reactions of fellow workers, knowing these responses is crucial to one's personal safety. This rite of passage may be informally sanctioned by the administration and seems to be enjoyed by the tenured workers as well as the prisoners.

Most workers report surprise at their first contact with prisoners. The direction of this surprise is not uniform. Some remark that the prison was much less forbidding than imagined while others comment on the visible tension of the prison. These first impressions are dependent on the changing atmosphere of the prison. For workers who enter the prison under lock down conditions, the prison appears to be a more restricted environment. As one lieutenant remarked, "They start now (during a lock down) and they never see a sea of inmates on the yard. They are always shocked when everyone is unlocked and they see inmates all over the place. It is hard for them to get used to after a long lock down." Howard (1980) also describes a new worker's reaction to an unlocked down yard:

Paul was relieved when his tour of the Row was over and they returned to the yard. But again, when they got outside, he was almost stunned by the sheer number of convicts everywhere. There were literally hundreds of them, all around him. He had known, of course, that there would be scores and scores of them, because after all, San Quentin was a prison; but for some reason he had imagined them locked up, not moving around all over the place, not gathering in groups in the yard, not milling about here, there, everywhere. It seemed that the entire inside of the prison was a seething montage of blue—with only an occasional dot of brown. "There are so many of them," he said, almost to himself (Howard, 1980, p. 116).

In the interviews for this study these first impressions were reported:

At first I was scared working at San Quentin, but after talking to the inmates I saw that they were not all assholes. A lot of convicts say there is no place like SQ and they prefer it, like I do.

I was unsure at first, I had read *The San Quentin Story* about Warden Duffy. There were a lot of killings and a lot of fights. The name, San Quentin, makes you think about that a lot. But after four or five months I mellowed and started figuring out what it was all about.

I didn't know anything about San Quentin. I felt that all the other officers were old-timers and that I would never fit in there as a young man.

The main thing that bothered me was that the cells were so small. I couldn't see how people could live in there. I expected to see people in worse conditions than they were. I thought they would look more hard— but they weren't all bad. These people are at home here. Some are more comfortable and secure here than they would be on the outside.

Ah shit, I thought look at those big old walls. It was a challenge to me then and it still is.

I had never been in a prison before. I wasn't really scared, I guess more nervous. The yard was tame then. I felt unprepared, I worked a gun position. There was no one there. You count the people at night. I was ready for a lot of action and there wasn't any. I just worked on my courage. Well, I guess you could say that I was scared at first.

It was scary and intense. A new person does not know about all the power, or understand how people in the different groups get the power. I felt covered with dirt when I walked into that place. You did not know how to deal with staff or inmates. Some of the staff would turn you loose and let you flounder . . . still it was a good learning experience. It has all changed now. Then you were scared to go back on the tier. There were some places that officers had no business being. In 1976 it was very scary.

These first impressions are an initial step in developing a world-view. The second step is grounded in the day-to-day contacts each officer makes going about the job. Glaser (1964) suggests that the nature of the specific job duties may determine worker attitudes toward prisoners:

The more ritualistic and routinized the duties of an employee become in dealing with an inmate, the more he is inclined to become authoritarian and punitive toward them, and the more he is inclined to rationalize punitiveness by stereotyping unfavorable conceptions of inmates and inmates are inclined to reciprocate with like responses (Glaser, 1964, p. 89).

This range of duty is related to both the kinds of prisoners locked up and the variety of encounters themselves. For a worker who is assigned to a more "benign" location in the institution, such as visiting or minimum security housing outside the main perimeter, relations with prisoners take on a less adversarial form. The interaction between worker and prisoner represents a pursuit of mutual goals and may not be antagonistic. In the more secure or more transient housing units, however, the lack of one-on-one interaction with prisoners creates experiences that may support impersonal definitions of the prisoners. Often, these contacts are neutral and may be based on long-term interaction. The following interchange between a veteran worker, Krasenes, and "prison revolutionary" George Jackson is suggested by Howard (1980):

Paul Krasenes came along the tier with a small stack of mail in his hands. Spain had one letter and a *Jet* magazine, which Paul put on the bars of his cell. When he got to George's cell, George was standing there, so he handed his mail to him. "How's it going, Jackson?" Paul asked. "Not bad," George replied, "not bad at all."

Krasenes and Jackson had known each other off and on for about five years. At one point in his prison career, George had been locked down in the AC for fifteen months, and had seen Krasenes on one shift or another five days a week. Hardly friendly, they had never, however, been antagonistic. As a matter of fact, Krasenes had even wished George good luck on his release after his fifteen-month lock down (Howard, 1980, p. 100).

Interaction with prisoners, through day-to-day contact and specific housing or job assignments, provides opportunity for intersections of interests. Recognizing that the delivery of meals, mail, escorts to visits or medical appointments serves both the interests of the worker (who desires to get through the day without hassle) and the prisoner (who is the ultimate recipient of these services) is the first step toward an intersection of interests. An examination of the job of the worker illustrates these contacts.

DUTIES OF THE PRISON WORKER

Understanding the reproduction of social control through the worldview of the worker requires a brief analysis of the job and its duties. The range of activities and tasks which make up the workday illustrate the demands of the role and the operation of power, meaning, interests, and interaction. The job varies tremendously and may depend on position, shift, and the approach of the individual performing these duties. Lombardo describes the stereotype that ignores the complications of the job:

The traditional portrait of the prison guard has him standing in the prison yard, nightstick in hand, or sitting in a tower with his machine gun, observing inmates as they go about their daily routine below (Lombardo, 1981, p. 38).

The reality of the job is more complex. Jacobs and Retsky (1975) list four basic groups: housekeeping, security, service delivery, and work supervision. Each of these duties provides opportunities for interaction among workers and prisoners and reveals interests and power arrangements.

Housekeeping tasks illustrate this dynamic. Prison workers assigned to housing units have a great deal of discretion over the form of these tasks. Under some conditions, a housing officer may have prisoner workers to help with these duties. The worker is responsible for the delivery of mail, supply of articles such as toilet paper, and the all-important tobacco and matches. If the tier is under lock down, delivering meals may also be part of this responsibility. Many times the scarce conditions of the prison leave the officer without sufficient supplies. Enterprising (and caring) officers may scavenge the needed supplies from another cell block, knowing that their tier will run much more smoothly with these high demand and necessary provisions.

On the other hand, officers who do not recognize the intersections of interest between worker and prisoner may not take such a personal responsibility for these provisions and may suffer the problems of an unruly tier. This intersection of interests and its recognition forms a potential for intimacy among the housing officer and his tier. One seasoned worker reports that he feels directly responsible for both the physical and the emotional condition of his tier when on duty. He feels that he makes every effort to "facilitate the smooth running of my tier, and I expect my prisoners to do the same." He reports that prisoners respond to this expectation and that he is proud of the fact that no incidents, such as assaults or fires, have ever occurred during his shift. Such earthy demands as supplying toilet paper to human beings demonstrate the dependent and reciprocal nature of the relationships between worker and prisoner.

Not all positions involve ongoing interaction with the same group of prisoners. The most obvious of these are gun rail and gun tower positions: "working the gun" or patrolling the perimeter of the prison. In addition, San Quentin has a special security squad that investigates gang activity and patterns of assault. Known within the prisoner culture as the Goon Squad, this small unit has special authority over workers as well as being responsible for investigating workers' infractions of rules.

Service delivery positions comprise another type of job. This includes distributing mail and meals to the prisoners, processing visitors and paperwork, receiving new prisoners and paroling those released to the outside. Much of the actual work involved in these services is done by the prisoners. Workers then are involved with supervision of the prisoners assigned to these tasks. Supervising prisoners who work in the kitchen, the laundry, maintenance, and the vocational areas of the prison provides another opportunity for recurring interaction between correctional workers and prisoners. Jacobs and Retsky (1975) and Sykes (1958) have noted the potential for normalized relations between the worker and the prisoner in the work situation. Relations among those working together seem to transcend the official status of officer and prisoner (Sykes, 1958). Here again there is a potential for intense interaction and the recognition of common interests. For example, the officer supervising a painting assignment will choose workers who share his or her concern with getting the job done. Additional informal perks are contained within job assignments for prisoners and are therefore desired by the prisoners. Reducing the boredom of imprisonment, introducing activity into the day, and other advantages are available to working prisoners. The kitchen, for example, can be a desired position since access to food and showers are some of the informal perks that come with this assignment. Officers supervising the work assignments need good workers to accomplish assigned tasks and prisoners want to keep a "bonaroo" job assignment. Like relations on the tier, work tasks provide for interaction and reciprocity between worker and prisoner.

ABUSE BY PRISONERS

There are, however, many interactions that do not form such an intersection. Verbal abuse and physical threats constitute experiences that parallel negative definitions of the prisoner and shape antagonisms between worker and prisoner. One of the most extreme contacts between workers and prisoners is known as "gassing," where prisoners throw substances from their cells onto the officer. These substances may be water, coffee, or food, but urine and feces are routinely used. Some officers report that they have never been gassed, while others found it a common occurrence in their early days on the job. The key determinant of one's chances of being gassed appear to be the extent of face-to-face interaction. For workers who have regular contact with specific prisoners, for example, distribute mail or meal trays and engage in light conversation during these contacts, gassing is a rare occurrence. For those who do not speak to the prisoners, or who have just transferred to the unit, gassing is more likely to occur. Most of the workers see gassing as an impersonal release of frustrations by the prisoners.

I was gassed during my first week on the job. The man mixed urine with detergents and oven cleaner. He threw it in my face, it burnt my eyes. I lost 5 percent of my vision. . . . Later I was told by the other inmates that he had been talking so much shit that he could not go out in the yard with them, so he did something to the staff. He had done it before. It's his thing. It was really traumatic for me. For days I tried to understand his perspective—it was just that he decided to lash out.

I would have gotten three days off for an injury, but I came right back. I was new and I didn't want to start off taking three days off. The inmates noticed that my eyes were burning and I think I got a lot of respect from the convicts for coming back. When it happened, they tried to tell me to watch out. After that, the sergeant put me on another tier, but I came back and the inmates told me what was going on then.

This incident illustrates a process through which prisoners who want to be separated from others will use an assault on an officer as a means to gain protective custody or other change in housing status. This is known as using an officer to "P. C." (gain protective custody). Because asking for protective custody is seen as "weak," prisoners may take this roundabout way to gain such protection. Generally, gassing, like other elements of worker-prisoner relations depends on the levels and degree of interaction. New workers, temporary workers, or those with "jackets" (reputations) of unfairness are the most likely ones to be assaulted in this way. Workers who have been in the same job or are personally known to most of the prisoners are very seldom gassed. Other prisoners may often warn a well-known officer of the possibility that someone may "go off" and become abusive or violent.

Verbal assaults also follow this pattern, but are much more common. Most workers report experiencing verbal assaults throughout their career in the Department of Corrections. Here, there appears to be some relationship between the custody level of the housing unit (where most verbal exchanges take place), the amount of interaction between workers and prisoners, and the amount of abuse. In minimum security housing units, gassing and verbal abuse are rare. In the higher custody units, verbal assaults are expected more and, in many ways, rationalized by the personal characteristics of the populations housed in them.

Race and sex also influence the amount of abuse one may encounter. Especially in the racially segregated lock up units, such action may be racially motivated. A new, black worker recalls having a cup of orange juice thrown on him by a member of the Aryan Brotherhood (AB), a white supremacist prison gang:

The guy was an AB, a real prejudiced inmate. I was pouring orange juice one morning and a little bit sloshed out and got on his hand. So he threw it at me and said, "Damn you nigger, what do you think you are doing?" and I threw the whole bucket on him. It was wrong, but it was just a reaction.

Another black officer says that early in his career, racial insults from white prisoners would cause him to lose his temper. At one point, he exploded, "Yeah, that's right. I'm a nigger, but just remember that this nigger feeds you." Now, after several years on the job, he says he would not respond so "unprofessionally." A female worker with six years experience suggests that women are more likely to be "cussed at" than gassed:

No, I have never been gassed. Maybe I have had little things thrown out of the cell at me. But I have never really been messed with that much. I usually get cussed at—that is constant. "Come and sit on this," "hey bitch." One of the new ones, I think it comes from LA, is "punk bitch." You hear things that you did not know existed in our vocabulary.

To tell you the truth, a lot of times it pisses me off. . . . I see a lot of female officers who turn around and respond to it but I don't see how you can [respond to it]. . . . Cuss them back? I think that just turns them on, they are doing that to get some kind of a reaction. I just look blank, and just keep on walking. It is really important to me to maintain my self-respect.

Beyond verbal assaults and gassing, the potential for physical assaults exists. Bowker (1980) suggests that the rate of physical assaults on officers has increased since the 1970s. He lists several "high risk activities"—breaking up fights, cell-transfers, shake-downs, and escorting prisoners to segregation units—which present the most potentially dangerous situations. Overall, however, Bowker argues that the chance of physical assault is minimal. The biggest dangers, he asserts, are psychological and suggests that manipulation, corruption of authority, verbal assaults, gassings, and threats against workers' families are the most systematically damaging. Even in a dangerous riot situation, Bowker suggests that the individual worker's relationship with prisoners may, in fact, determine the potential for personal harm. Park (1976) found that increased violence has been associated with greater deliberateness and ideological rhetoric of prisoners. Like others (Bennett, 1976), Park ties increased prison violence for the radicalization of California's prisoners.

In the perspective of the "old-timer" [worker], relations with prisoners were more free in "the old days." The increased bureaucratization, court scrutiny, and legal constraints are perceived to undermine this. Bob Powers tells this story:

One day this guy gave me a real hard time about coffee. I was serving hot coffee on the tiers and he kept saying that he didn't want any and then he would want some, and back and forth. Finally he took his cup and threw it back on me. I just looked at him and said, "You should not have done that." I finished serving and walked back to the cart. Everybody on the tier saw what happened and was waiting to see what was next. I took some coffee, some syrup, all kinds of things and mixed it up in a big can and walked back down and threw the whole mess on him. I was very careful not to get it on his bed, his personal stuff or his paperwork. Then I asked him what size clothes he wore, and got him a dry set of clothes and towels to clean up with. The whole tier saw me walk down the tier and no one warned him that I was coming. Never had any trouble with him again.

Then years later, I was working North Block and he was living there. The guy living right next door to him started the same thing—threatening to throw stuff on me. . . . I asked him if he wanted coffee and he said no. The guy next to him, the guy from AC, said, "Hey brother, just take the coffee, the rest of us want coffee." So I gave him a cup and continued down the tier. When I got up on the next tier, I could hear these turkeys talking . . . the guy from AC said, "Hey that cop is crazy, you don't want to fuck with him." If I did that today, I'd probably be written up and given 10 days off as a disciplinary.

JUICE: A UNIQUE FORM OF POWER

A special category of prisoners may have what is described as "juice." While related to the concept of respect, "juice" is related to formal and informal power arrangements. In the controlled environment of the prison, the prisoner or the worker who can assert individual will is seen to have juice. Discovering that a prisoner may have more power and influence than an officer is part of the socialization into the culture of the pen. Juice generally follows the traditions of race and sex, especially in the particularized "dad and kid" relationships between workers and prisoners. In terms of race, almost all "dad and kid" relationships take place within the same race. Women workers, however, face special obstacles in their interaction with the male prison community. A relationship between a female worker and a male prisoner is almost always suspect. Their relations with male workers are no less troublesome. Women are seen, even by other women workers, to use sexual favors to get ahead. Because of this suspicion, and the lack of women in high places, few female workers have specialized relationships with prisoners.

Juice can be seen as an extreme form of respect. Like respect, it is based on personal qualities, patterns of interaction, and personalized relationships that have developed over time. One worker describes "juice inmates":

[Juice inmates] have been around a long time. They are in with a top sergeant or lieutenant or an administrator that has juice. They can pretty much do what they want as long as it is not in the extreme. The longer they are around, the more they get. It is just like the way an officer gets juice. Happens the exact same way; you build up friendships and you learn to take advantage of friendships. I sort of resent convicts that can go over my head. It isn't supposed to work that way. But no one guarantees the way things will work.

While juice may be a public quantity, other forms of personalized relationships are often kept quiet. Two of these forms are what Irwin (1980) calls "corrupt favoritism and personal agreement." Many relationships of this type are grounded in both interaction and a level of friendship. While few workers will describe their overall relationships with prisoners as a "friendship," most will admit they like some individuals more than others. These workers claim they take special steps to conceal this preference, at least publicly. Part of respect involves recognizing this reciprocity of roles. Sykes argues this reciprocity is crucial to the maintenance of order. The following example illustrates this interdependence:

I was working in the AC at night and some guys were really playing their radios too loud. The sergeant comes in and tells me to make them cut them off. Well, I approach them with a request, an order isn't going to get me anywhere. I tell these guys that the sergeant is really on my ass about noise and would they just turn it down for awhile. They usually recognize that I am going to have to ride them until the noise level goes down so they are pretty good about it. They also know that the sergeant will just come in and cut off all the electricity to their cells so they at least keep it down when he is on the block.

Another aspect of this reciprocity concerns the exchange of information. While every version of the prison code contains some prohibition against informing (or being a "rat," a "stool pigeon," or "rolling over") the exchange of information between individual workers and prisoners is commonplace. Even seasoned prisoners who cultivate a "right guy" image will share information with workers they respect. Information that may damage one's friends is not usually conveyed, but dropping a kite on an enemy or competitor occurs more often than "right guys" will admit. Anonymous information is part of the prison grapevine, but very often workers will receive information about planned "hits" (stabbings or assaults) from prisoners who trust them. One veteran worker says this often puts her in a bind as she worries about her ability to protect the confidence of her informant:

I get all kinds of information from my workers [prisoners] but I have no way of giving that information to [other] staff without giving them up. They [staff] know the inmates that I talk to and I do not trust my sergeant at all so I just keep those things to myself. When they tell me something big, I really need to go tell somebody but if I can't protect them I will not tell.

Other workers tell of a sergeant refusing to accept the credibility of such information by saying "Oh, the inmates are just trying to get in good with you. Don't believe everything they tell you." Workers feel that this reaction discourages communication among staff and further contributes to levels of alienation.

There is some evidence that workers may share information with individual prisoners. If a sweep of a cell block is planned, workers may let prisoners with whom they have a personalized relationship know beforehand. However, if the prisoner does not heed the warning, and contraband is discovered in the cell, few workers will attempt to hide the evidence. A central part of each worker's privatized worldview is the fine line between doing a favor and not doing one's duty. Each worker may see this line differently, again contributing to conflicts in definitions of the job and contradictions in worldviews.

Part of the prisoner/worker reciprocity involves "watching the back" of a worker. Particularly in potentially dangerous situations, prisoners may come to the aid of the worker. The following two stories illustrate this. Bob Powers recalls the first time a prisoner came to his assistance:

One day I was trying to get the men to lock up . . . what we used to do is walk up to them and say "Ok, let's lock up" and they would break up and go to their cells. One day I was yelling lock up and the black inmates did not want to break up. I'd walk up to them and they would just look at me, and keep talking to each other. Just ignore me. Pretty soon I realized that I was being surrounded by a circle of black inmates and I did not know what was going to happen. I felt someone bump up against my back and I did not know who it could be . . . an officer or what. So I turned around and it was A——[prisoner]. He had been around a long time, he was huge, he could bench press 300 pounds. He just looked at me and I did not know what was going to happen and he said to me, "Don't worry Mr. Powers, these guys will lock up," and he said, "OK boys, let's do what the man says," and they did. I have always had a lot of respect for him and I guess he had a lot for me.

[Why?] Well, I guess it is because I always talk to everybody. I let them know who I am, give them a cigarette if I have one. Whatever, I try not to shine them on.

Some workers report that prisoners give them information for their own protection. Generally this warning is to keep them from walking into something that might get them hurt. "Hey, C—— don't go back there, run and get some help."

One officer, for example, says if she trusts the prisoner from past contact, she will get help rather than attempt to handle something on her own. Another female worker, on probation, has the opposite reaction:

I have inmates actually physically restrain me and tell me not to run to that alarm. I say, "What is wrong with you, move out of my way." And they tell me that there is enough help, that I should just stay here out of the shit. I know they are just looking out for me. But it makes me sort of mad because this is the kind of thing that I have been waiting for all this time, to make it to the alarm and to get in on the excitement. I thank them for their concern but I tell them that this is my job, this is what I am here for and that if I am up on the gun and they start something then I will shoot them.

Even within the atmosphere of increased tensions, interaction remains fundamental to the prison social order. Despite the official prohibitions against "fraternization" and familiarity, workers and prisoners develop relationships out of ongoing interaction on the shop floor of the prison. These relationships can be based on a long-time job assignment in the unit, a reputation that comes from being on the job for some time, or previous contacts in other parts of the prison. Unless there are grounds for personal animosity from these previous encounters, these relationships appear to endure over time. For some veteran workers, relations with certain prisoners can span many years. In a special type of the "dad and kid" relationship, workers, particularly those with "juice" or position, may look after a prisoner whom they have known since their "fish" days. It is possible to find workers who have known individual prisoners for ten or fifteen years and who have developed a friendship based on trust and respect. A prisoner with a "dad" in high place may receive special treatment. This relationship becomes common knowledge, and is acknowledged by workers and prisoners alike. While such a close friendship may resemble the identification of interests known as fraternizing, this relationship is protected by the position, status or juice of the worker (generally a superior officer) and by the "right guy" reputation of the prisoner. (The liability for such a relationship also affects the prisoner. Being too cozy with "the man" in many circumstances may appear to imply an informant relationship. But among dads and kids, such a relationship is protected by the status of both parties).

Dads and kids are a special form of such relations among workers and prisoners, but, along with gassing, illustrate the possible range of such relations. The key elements of this range are interaction and the context of encounters. The gassed worker generally has no "track record" with prisoners and the dad and kid have a long history of positive personal encounters. Within this range are the majority of relations with prisoners. Some interactions are basically antagonistic, while others are wholly positive. The ways in which interaction, distribution of power, and the definitions of the situation serve to structure relations with prisoners are revealed in these typologies.

PRISONER TYPOLOGIES

Throughout the workday, the prison worker comes into contact with all types of prisoners. Most workers have a specific set of images they use to sort these experiences and can describe categories or types of prisoners. The most general typing involves some sort of continuum. A basic typology ranges from "asshole" to "all right convict," with "respect" underpinning these categories. As a reflexive property, a prisoner gets respect from an officer when the prisoner shows the same respect toward the worker. At times, the worker may be tested to determine whether respect is deserved, but once it is accorded, respect seems to persist. As with many prison terms, respect is somewhat difficult to define. Generally, respect refers to a personal quality of fairness and consistency and may be both symbolic and actual. In the prison, respect is crucial toward sustaining relations, and may also sustain the personal authority of the workers.

In the "asshole—all right" continuum, the asshole does not give respect and therefore does not receive it. The all right convict both gives and receives respect. Respect also implies some kind of shared understanding about the social order of the prison. Respect acknowledges the roles of the worker and the prisoner, and, at the same time, transcends them. Many workers and prisoners tell of one-on-one encounters where the roles of authority and power disappear. In Sykes's (1958) explanation of these reciprocal roles, the worker and the prisoner may approach each other as individuals rather than as the keeper and the kept. For the worker, the prisoner who can distinguish between this front stage and backstage performance (Goffman, 1961a) is one who can be respected. Respect can also be generated outside of official expectations. Although a given behavior may be prohibited (for example, a stabbing), such behavior may be respected when it suits the situation. The best examples of this are "incidents" where one prisoner assaults another. Such circumstances of self-protection, especially in the case of attempted rape by another prisoner, are tacitly understood and tolerated by the correctional worker. These incidents represent another double bind for the worker. Given an understanding of the prison codes, the worker can see the necessity of such action, even though it violates the rules and disturbs the desired peace of the shift. A tough prisoner, who "won't take any shit" from anyone is respected by prisoners and workers:

Boy, this is a really bad thing for staff to say, but I will tell you this because I think even the warden would admit this. The last thing we want an inmate to do is ask for Protective Custody. See, on the streets I have legal avenues to protect myself. The guy in here does not have any recourse to protect himself from the other inmates. He is here with us, and when I put on the uniform this guy becomes my responsibility. This guy has to walk the mainline here. However, when the pressure is so great, whether it is for sex, for canteen, pressuring you or the family, if the guy has got to take a piece and do his number, then let him. Otherwise we are going to have to lock everyone up in PC units.

"Respect" also allows the prisoner to be defined as more human, and most importantly, more of a "man'" in the macho culture of the prison. The prisoner who is respected, will get respect. The prisoner who is disrespected, or who shows disrespect, falls in the category of "asshole" and, in the words of the culture, has "nothing coming." Without respect, the prisoner may be subjected to the petty to serious oppressions that are available to the correctional worker. With respect, the prisoner may enjoy fair treatment from other prisoners and most workers.

It is not always possible for each worker to know each prisoner, particularly under the current conditions of crowding and high staff turnover. So while respect is primary to this interaction, other systems of typing are used by the worker. While some workers deny that race affects their relations with prisoners, most admit that it becomes a factor in the racially charged atmosphere of San Quentin. Women workers have special problems with the racial issue. They report that prisoners react to this combination of race and gender. One white woman reports that she has little trouble with black prisoners and the majority of hassles come from whites, who she says, see her as a "traitor to the race." The general sentiment toward race is expressed by a new worker, "It is the simplest way to categorize people; it makes the job easier. If you have a stabbing between the blacks and the whites, you lock up all whites and blacks. If it is between two whites, then you lock up the whites."

A black male officer, who has worked in several California prisons says:

Everything here is segregated. I hate to talk like this because in a way it is talking against the system. This is almost a radical statement, but it is what I believe. The prison emphasizes race among the inmates and it breeds among the staff too, I know they think that if the inmates are fighting among themselves, then they won't be fighting the staff. . . . They emphasize—white cell, black cell.

[Do the prisoners react to that?] They are so full of hatred that they don't recognize the manipulation, the segregated housing and the ethnically balanced policy. It is manipulation. The blacks say, "Look at what the white boys are getting" and then the whites say, "Look what those toads are getting." I hate to say this, but I would really rather see them doing that to each other than to us. It is a way of surviving here.

PRISON CULTURE

Prison culture can be thought of as an organization of experience and interactions. Through the lens provided by this culture, relations with prisoners can be seen in terms of two historically evolved conceptions: "convicts" and "inmates." Workers see a distinction between "convicts" and "inmates" and between older prisoners and "youngsters." The categorizing of convicts and inmates reflects a change in the definition of prisoners that was brought on by the use of the rehabilitative ideal. Prisoners became "inmates" under this new definition of imprisonment (Fogel, 1979). For the older workers, a nostalgia for the old days colors their version of prison/worker relations. A veteran with 20 years experience tells of the old days when a prisoner could have "one of the bulls on the yard act as his P.O. (parole officer)." If a prisoner was locked up for disciplinary reasons, for example, thrown in the hole (housed in the adjustment center), the personalized relations between worker and prisoner often were used as a basis for "speaking up" for someone. Part of this nostalgia for the old days is related to the previous power arrangements between worker and prisoner. Before the courts became actively involved in prisoner rights, (Yee,

1973; Fogel, 1979) the tyranny of personalized relationship determined a prisoner's "rights." Under current judicial review, such constitutional rights as due process have weakened the discretionary power of the worker. Many workers, both young and old, see "interference from the courts" as a central problem of the institution. In the interviews, court scrutiny is seen negatively. The courts are perceived by workers not to "understand the problems of the prison" and to apply "half-baked," liberal solutions to their problems. The primary criticism of these court decrees involves their unenforceability. Workers do not see the practical applications of these solutions based on abstract, legal principles. Additionally, these nostalgic versions of prisoners relate to the former systems of discretion and inequality. Fogel describes this discretion in discussing the power of a warden:

Inside the walls his discretion reigned supreme, but it looked odd when it had to be explained in a courtroom. The prisoner as plaintiff enjoys the status of "equality" before the bench. The judge was not likely to listen as sympathetically to . . . James Park, Associate Warden of San Quentin (1971), explaining how he knew his culprit:

That's simple; we knew who did it from the other inmates. . . . If several reliable inmates point to this guy, or refuse to clear him, then we know he is guilty. We don't have the type of case we could take to court; it would be too dangerous for our inmate informers to testify. You middle class due-processors don't understand it is an administrative matter, not judicial (Fogel, 1979, p. 169).

Many workers see explicit differences in the actions between younger and older prisoners. Depending on the degree of penetration into the prison culture, the worker may use the convention of prison numbers to explain these differences. These numbers give the savvy worker a clue to a prisoner's position into the prison culture in terms of age and experience. One officer with six years of experience uses these categories:

Well, the man in blue would rather be called a convict; an inmate is the way almost everybody refers to them now. A "C" number is a younger man, prone to be more violent and has less prison experience. A "B" number guy has done time, depending on how high the number is. An "A" number guy is definitely in for murder. A's and B's are mellowed out, a senior citizen group. Late C's and D's are the younger guys. They are wild and they have to prove it right now.

Again, respect is the key to these definitions. Younger prisoners are seen as lacking respect for anything, including other prisoners. The older prisoners are perceived to have "figured out" what doing time is about (that is, distribution of power and respect) and to have some attachment to the prisoner code. George Elliot gives this example:

Back in the old days, I hate to keep saying the old days, but that's how it is thought of . . . back when I first started if you [prisoner] were drinking and saw a cop coming, you would straighten up and play it off. With these new guys, they don't even care. [They say] I have been drinking and if you think you are bad enough to try and come in here, just try it . . . but in the old days the old-timers would play it off, and say, "Hey, how are you doing Officer Elliot;" you could just smell it all over and they'd keep talking, how's the family, how's everything going, and you would just grin because you know the guy was up to something . . . and it was kind of funny because it was nothing major. The guy was keeping it to himself. Now the young guys drink beyond their limit and they start acting stupid and doing dumb things.

A perceptive newcomer to the prison work talks about the need for worker and prisoner to "save face":

You have shit and piss thrown on you, guys who snivel to you all the time. And you might happen to find out that this guy wasted a 93-year-old lady or something like that. There is a certain amount of resentment that builds up over time. And then you see this old-timer, an A number come in and this guy never asks you for anything and that is great. Then a B number who never asks you for anything and that is terrific. And then you have these damn little C numbers and all they do is snivel. What they may fail to realize is that punishment is confinement, nothing more, nothing less. I am not here to administer any further forms of punishment, that is not my job. But these younger guys do not realize that as long as they leave an officer alone, nothing will happen to them. An A number and some of the B's sure know that. Stay out of the officer's face, don't create situations where the officer has to save face with other inmates or with other officers. The same way the inmate has to save face, the officer has to save face as well. Because if he does not hold his ground on the tier everything will blow up. He is weak, he is very weak.

A ten-year veteran worker sees that convicts were more predictable in the old days because they know exactly "what they had coming." He argues that it is not so much the individuals who have changed, but rather that the system itself had modified these relations:

In the old days, I could learn what their little foibles and games were. I could communicate with them on a one-to-one basis. If they called "hey S____[nickname] I knew who it was. He'd say, "Hey my stomach hurts, call the MTA," and I would know if he had a legitimate gripe. They would know that if I told them something I would do it, everything within the authority of my position and sometimes beyond that. They were in that unit with me long enough so we had a degree of familiarity and respect. Now there is no familiarity, there is only contempt. They try and steal food from that mess hall right in front of you, five years ago they would at least wait until you have turned your back.

The system has changed. They can get away with more. [With the workers] it is mostly lack of experience, job knowledge, and authority. I used to be able to work with a convict. I could take something from him, and he would know that if he did it again and he got caught with me he would get what he had coming because I gave him a play last time.

They would know that they could go so far and they couldn't exceed it. The limits for the inmates are gone. They get away with what they can get away with. And they keep trying more all the time.

A worker with a family history in prison work has a more historical perspective on the split between older and younger prisoners:

The thing that is really sad is that the State of California does not know how to deal with these youngsters. The old-timer had a legitimate beef;

there were a lot of things wrong [in the old system]. I can remember things that my dad used to tell me, that my cousins used to tell me . . . all kinds of constitutional things that don't go on today. These old-time [prisoners] earned these [new rights] . . . but there have been a lot of problems that have come of these changes . . . and we don't know how to deal with them. Because we have a new breed of inmates that are taking advantage of them . . . without understanding where [the rights] stem from.

These new guys coming in here never had to live with the old system and they are abusing it [the rights]. When they slam this place down for good, these creative guys are going to think about it and someone, somewhere is going to have a light bulb turn on and say, "Wait a minute, I can win this" and they will, right here in this county. They will learn to build on these tools and we will have a less secure institution, there will be a lot of holes [because of these challenges to the law]. It will be wide open to those less scrupulous inmates, the ones that are less moralistic than the old-timers.

As older, more stable prisoners parole or transfer out due to lower custody ratings, the status of the old-timer may assume the dimensions of another prison myth. A nostalgia for the "good old days" maintains existing power relations without threatening the negotiated perspectives of the veteran workers. Allowing an abstract, positive version of old prisoners also legitimizes existing systems of informal power distribution. Sustaining one category of prisoners as the "good" prisoner allows for discretionary treatment and sanctions the privatized worldview of the correctional worker.

Snitches and Protective Custody

While snitching can be seen as proof the convict code is weakening, the code itself is most probably part of the prisoner's ideology of power and in fact was rarely practiced in its pure form. Many prisoners see the code as a "lie" and come to recognize the code's ability to manipulate power arrangements among the prisoners. Snitches are distrusted and seen as weak. The weak prisoner presents a variety of problems for the worker. Weak prisoners may require protection from other prisoners and create a management problem for the institution. Most prisons have protective custody sections, where prisoners in need of protection are separated completely from the mainline and lock up populations. Among the prisoners, the person who "locks up" is generally defined as weak and incapable of "holding his mud." In the prisoner culture, once a person is in protective custody, he is defined as "less than a man" and subject to victimization upon his release. Many prisoners who enter protective custody are there for the rest of their term. Debts, sexual attacks, informing, or being a former law enforcement officer are some of the reasons for granting or requiring protective custody.

Other images of the prisoner relate to a particularized worldview. One veteran worker, who works primarily in the Adjustment Center, divides prisoners by "those who have it coming and those who do not." He recognizes the abilities of the prisoners to perceive the injustices of their situations:

You have to admire some of these guys. They can nail you to the wall when you are wrong and you know they are right. This kind of guy will begin to get some kind of power, some kind of respect from everybody. Respect is the most important thing here. Your word then is worth a whole lot.

Respect remains central to the definition of the prisoner. Many workers see that.

The old-timers have done most of their time and they are just waiting to get to the streets. They do not need to prove themselves by being violent or assaultive. The younger people are still into killing to prove themselves.

A convict respects you and your job. He knows that you are only doing your job. He doesn't make it a personal thing. An inmate is a youngster that has no respect for anybody.

A key part of this respect is not bothering anybody—prisoners or workers. Most workers recognize that most prisoners have some kind of hustle going (William and Fish, 1974), but resent the prisoner who "fronts them off":

The one that wants to do his time without trying to hassle me, that's the good kind of convict. I am sure all of them have rackets going, but as long as it does not hurt anybody, it's ok with me. That's the thing that gets to me the most about this job—I can't stand to see anybody hurt, even if I don't like them. And I'll tell you, I don't like most of them in here. [Sometimes I am standing around] and I see someone go by three or four times and I will tell them, "Look, I know you are running something, but I don't want to know about it as long as it will not hurt anybody." Because if it does, it might be my back, or another officer or an inmate. And I do not want to see that. I am sure that they all have their little things, but as long as it does not hurt anybody physically then it is ok with me. But they all want to talk like they are the big man or something. I have told them, I am sure you were the big man where you came from, maybe in your home town, but here you are just another inmate.

A new worker, with only four months on the job has little am-bivalence in her negative definition of the prisoners. But her at-titude indicates a gap between her personal views and those she claims to be part of the professionalism of the job.

I see them all as scam artists. Their job is to lie to you and your job is to catch them. It is schizophrenic for me because I treat them a lot different than the way I feel about them. Inside, I never forget the victims. If I am joking around with them and shooting the shit, acting real cool, I know in the back of my head that someone is either dead or in bad shape because of these people. I also know that this guy would turn around, in a second, and rape me bloody and slit my throat. They will turn on you in a minute. In a mob situation, all of them would.

I had an experience the other day in the so-called honor block, the supposed honor unit, quote, unquote. Well those guys are no different than anybody else. There I am real cool, I get along basically with everybody. "Hey, how's it going" to everybody I see. Well there was a bad storm and the window blew open, and I went down to lock the window and the whole goddamn side of the block went nuts. Calling me a whore and a tramp. And I just thought, Whoa, it's mob behavior . . . maybe it is their release but I was really taken aback. It brought me to the reality that "you guys ain't no fucking different either." So I just sat in the chair and said, "You got nothing coming from me." Why should I even try to be nice to you. You turn around and stab me in the back . . . it was totally disrespectful and I did not expect that from them. Maybe in the lock up units but not there.

An administrator who is no longer with the department does not see the usefulness of these distinctions among prisoners.

I don't see a big change . . . they want to be treated as people; they want respect, love, they want you to like them, they want understanding, and they want sex, too. We have changed the parameters through which all that can be given. They have gotten a little bit younger and more confused. They have more problems now because we give them more to worry about. They want a TV, a stereo, family visits. All this increases the anxiety level, just like on the outside.

Face-to-Face Interaction

Unlike past demands of the prison code, it appears that workers talk regularly with the prisoners. One veteran of 19 years at San Quentin says this started to happen somewhere in the 1970s. He tells of

"shooting the breeze with a prisoner" where the prisoner says, "You know, two or three years ago I would not be sitting here talking to you B_____, I would answer you if you said something and that was it." Before you would not fraternize with them for nothing. You would use their number and that was it. Never their nickname.

At one point during the racial tensions of the 1970s, there was little conversation across racial lines for workers and prisoners. Partly due to the changing image of the job, and due to the influence of women workers, conversations appear to be more commonplace. The decreased influence of the convict code may also account for these interactions. Workers report that these conversations with prisoners cover every possible subject. Prisoners are interested in hearing details of the street—especially details of workers' sex lives. With male workers, these conversations resemble standard locker room talks. Other aspects of the officers' personal lives are also explored. Some officers relax and discuss their outside lives with the prisoners, others refuse to do so. Still others say they "bullshit" the guys into believing they are having a really wild time out there. One officer convinced his tier of his romantic and adventuresome exploits to the extent that he was getting quite a reputation with the other workers as well. When an officer asked him if he really did all those things, he realized that the prison grapevine covered all members of the prison community, workers as well as prisoners.

Workers and prisoners also discuss their respective personal problems. One veteran officer who is perceived to have juice tells about his marriage break up and the way in which his contact with prisoners helped him get through a very difficult time.

When I was going through my divorce, these guys [prisoners] kept me going. They would make me eat in the kitchen, otherwise, I would not eat. I really care about these guys because of that . . . I worked on the lower yard . . . that was a really good place to work because I was around people all the time. The inmates were very important to me at that time. It was a perfect divorced man's job. If I wanted to be around people then I could, or if I wanted to be alone I could. After you have seniority here, you build up a rapport with these guys and they are very sympathetic, they would give me worlds of encouragement when I needed it. Once again, I started to look forward to coming to work. This is what kept me going. San Quentin was my life, I had nothing outside the gates. I thought about doing myself in one time . . . my rifle was right there.

Prisoners also discuss their personal problems with the workers, and many times the particular relationship determines the worker's reaction. Most of these conversations concern wives and girlfriends. If the prisoner has been an "all right" guy, then most workers will talk about the problem openly. But if the prisoner has "fucked with me," then the worker may respond by saying "you know she is running around on you, that is what you get for being in prison." Female workers are often asked for the "women's point of view." The officer's response will depend on her individual view of that prisoner. Women are also asked questions about their sex lives and none of the women interviewed here suggested that they encourage or acknowledge this topic. Some report they get mad and leave, while others joke it off and change the subject.

Workers were careful to point out the limits of conversations with prisoners. These workers were highly conscious of the role limits provided by the formal structure of the prison. One female worker says that you can only "talk to them on a certain level. I think most of my conversations with the inmates are shuck and jive . . . except, of course, the ones that have shown me they are made of something." Another worker, with nine years experience suggests that he "only trusts them half way":

Well sometimes I trust them and again I am always on my toes. I have trusted inmates before and I have gotten burnt. I do trust them to a certain extent but I am always leery. There were inmates that when I first started, they burned me bad, they stabbed me in the back. But I will trust them again, but within limits. I have to be on my guard with them. It comes down to knowing them over time, and having a good rapport with them. And maybe they have done me a favor in the past and they have the trust coming.

Idealized Relationships

In the interviews, workers constructed the characteristics of the "ideal" worker and his/her relationships with prisoners. The dimensions of this ideal are as follows:

• Don't lie to prisoners. The worker who makes promises and doesn't deliver is disrespected by both workers and prisoners. Such false promises endanger others. When a worker "sells wolf tickets" (makes promises he or she can't keep), the next worker has to deal with the broken promise.

• Treat them like you want to be treated. While this is tied to the reflexive nature of respect, it also indicates a specific definition of the prisoner as an equal human being. "Trying to understand the guy's predicament" was central to this dimension.

- Listen. Workers suggest that the ability to listen to an inmate is critical to the development of working relations. Again this involves a concept of the prisoner that emphasizes one's humanness and individuality.

- Be fair, and try to do what is right. The notion of consistency is always stressed as an important part of the job. This is one case in which the formal and the informal versions of the world overlap.

Interaction with prisoners individually, or in small stable groups, is most conducive to developing these definitions. Not all workers have that opportunity to come to know the prisoners on a face-to-face basis. As one top administrator who has come up through the ranks over the past 25 years says:

You have to understand that much of the job is treating prisoners in a mass. When you have to deal with a large group of people it is easy to see them as a big bunch without any individuality. I think that is the biggest problem for the correctional officer. He tends to define everybody in terms of the lowest common denominator and that causes a lot of problems.

The ability to "treat people like people" depends on defining them as such. Without close interactions which construct such a definition, the prisoner remains defined as part of this abstract mass. Thus, the worker's typology of prisoners is grounded specifically in the prison culture. Respect, race, and other cultural dimensions such as "old-timers vs. youngsters," convicts and inmates, and those who "have it coming" shape workers perceptions of prisoners. These typologies are also tied to relations workers develop with prisoners and the extent of their penetration into prison culture. As a worker becomes socialized into this culture, new definitions of the world and its members serve to construct typologies of prisoners. These typologies, in turn, generate actions toward prisoners and the reproduction of prison social organization.

CONCLUSION

Relations among prisoners and workers are grounded in the range of interests. These interests intersect and overlap in ways expected

and unexpected. Mutual goals, such as keeping the peace, avoiding violence, sharing information, and accomplishing such tasks as delivery of meals and mail, processing visits, or job assignments, shape relations among workers and prisoners. These relations, both positive and negative, illustrate quite concretely the dynamics of prison social organization and its dependence on a normative order grounded in respect, weakness, power, and specific versions of justice and fairness. Thus relations with prisoners are more complex than a surface investigation suggests. While workers may hold the power in a theoretical sense, examination of the concrete social order suggests that interaction, and the informal distribution of power serve to inform these relations with prisoners. The ways in which encounters develop into relationships, and the nature of these relationships mirror the reflexive nature of the prison social order. These relations thus become the foundation for the development of the worldview of the correctional worker and the subjective penetration—and subsequent reproduction—into the mechanisms of social control.

4

Relations Among Coworkers

Relations with coworkers are more complicated than relations with the prisoners and are characterized by the conflicts described in Chapter 2. While relations with prisoners are limited by the power distinctions between the two roles, relations among the correctional workers are more negotiable. These relations are shaped by a competition for this power and for scarce material and social resources, such as prestige, reputation, preferred days off, promotions, and desirable positions. These relations illustrate the subtle operation of social control as produced among the workers in their ongoing relations. Combining traditions of racism and sexism with competition, social control is introduced reflexively on the staff itself. The constraints on individual behavior by these relations demonstrate the way in which the worker is subjected to the very social control he attempts to reproduce in his relations with prisoners. Forces generated by the formal social organization of the prison, such as employer-employee relations and the paramilitary structure of the job, provide a normative order of codified rules and regulations. Beyond this formal social control lies a range of forces on the prison shop floor which also constrain and shape behavior.

Structurally, the conflicts are determined by the contradictory goals of the prison. Institutionally, these conflicts are shaped by

Portions of this chapter appeared as "Race and Gender among Prison Workers," *Crime and Delinquency*, vol. 31, no. 1, January 1985.

the degree of penetration into the reproductive mechanisms of authority. Personally, each officer is placed in competition with all other workers for the scarce resources and rewards of the prison. The combinations of these conflicts force each worker to resolve these problems on a day-to-day basis. These practical problems of getting through the day are the foundation of relations with fellow workers.

These conflicts are also grounded in a hierarchical power structure based on a semi-military bureaucracy. The formal access to these power structures is limited by promotional mechanisms, but a complex network of informal avenues creates keen competition among workers who pursue this power. The development of an elite, through cliques and personalized relationships distributes this informal power unequally. Conflicts in definitions of the job and of the nature of the work further divide the workers and provide a framework of distrust as well as competition. The emergence of camaraderie and team spirit among some workers combats these divisions but structural barriers often undermine these efforts toward worker cohesion. Traditional definitions of the "new breed of worker" which includes a high proportion of minority and women workers, combined with the definition of "fish" further divides the workers. At the time of the fieldwork, about 80 percent of workers have had less than one year employment in the prison. The consequence of this high turnover rate magnifies the problem of trust and cohesiveness, further aggravating the structural and personal divisions among the staff.

RACE AND SEX IN THE PEN

The worker culture was bound previously by a white, male version of the world. With the advent of affirmative action hiring requirements the more homogeneous guard force has been integrated by women and minorities. Although some changes in the composition of the administration of both California Department of Corrections and at San Quentin have occurred, the power structure of white, male administration continues. In the early 1980s, San Quentin received a black warden, one who had not advanced through the traditional custody ranks. This change in administration caused some shift in the existing formal power relations, particularly in terms of the ethnicity of the power structure. The effects of this shift were not discernible at the time of the fieldwork. Thus, the discussion below reflects the traditional perspective.

As noted by Jacobs (1977), the guard force traditionally has been white, male, sometimes rural, and experienced in military or other law enforcement backgrounds. Previously, the job paid a low wage. Currently, in California prisons, the pay scale has increased to make employment in a prison a relatively well-paying job (starting at $26,000 a year). Combined with the affirmative action policies, the harsh unemployment picture for most other jobs, the low entrance requirements (high-school education and two years work experience of any kind), and the increasingly "professional" image of the "correctional officer," the prison receives applications from people with diverse backgrounds and education. Approximately half of those interviewed for this study had some college background, many with an A.A. or B.A. degree. This shift from a homogeneous guard force to a heterogeneous group on all levels has had many effects on the culture of the guard force and on the prison as an institution.

At the time of the research, the guard force was predominantly male (approximately 80 percent) and the ethnic distribution for correctional workers was 55 percent white, 33 percent black, and 8 percent Chicano ("other" was the remaining 4 percent). Comparing this to the ethnic distribution of sergeants, the whites make up the majority (75 percent), blacks (17 percent), and Chicanos 3 percent ("other" make up the remaining 4 percent). The hiring policies have introduced race and sex as critical variables in the relationships and the interests of the line staff, and have had significant effects on all aspects of the prison culture.

Race

Among the prisoners, race has been a central feature of the prison social order. When minority workers were introduced into the prison, racial conflicts entered the worker culture as well.

Sobell (1974) describes his experience with a black worker in a federal penitentiary.

The officer I worked for was quite human. He was a black man with some college education, who had been sent down to the penitentiary shortly after the war as the first black officer. He didn't even last two weeks; the other officers, hacks and lieutenants alike, drove him off. . . . It was stupid of the Bureau to have sent a black down without first making sure of the reception he would get from the other hacks (Sobell, 1974, p. 252).

The shift to a more heterogeneous work force affects both relations among workers and between prisoners and the line staff. The racial segregation that characterizes prisoner social life (Carroll, 1977) also affects interactions among the workers and with the prisoners. With the prisoners, this separation has been voluntary, for example, segregation on the yard, in the chow halls, and in voluntary double-celling. Some job assignments also seem to be made along racial lines. With the current reality of racial gangs (Porter, 1982) and the dangerous warfare of these groups, the administration has segregated gang members in separate housing units or tiers. Critics of the prison suggest the administration encourages these racial hostilities as a way of confining hostilities and aggression to the prisoners and away from the staff (Irwin, 1980). Although the violence potential is missing from race relations among the staff, racial conflicts and competition occur among the staff as they do among the prisoners.

The racial conflict among the staff takes several general forms. The first is found in a response to the recent hiring practices. The white old-timers express resentment toward the affirmative action trends, but are careful not to describe this resentment in terms of race or gender, but in terms of "standards." A white male with six years experience offers this statement:

The big thing now is that they are hiring Chicans [prison slang for Chicano, also used by Chicanos themselves]. I am not saying that everybody in that race is crazy or stupid . . . I have worked with some very good officers who were Chicano. . . . I try to take every one, officers and inmates as a person. . . . I will use the racial cliches, whether they are black, white or whatever, "stupid nigger," "crazy spic." See that is just the way it is in there, it is part of the language in there. I just mean it to be derogatory toward that person, not the whole race. There are blacks that I don't like and then there are blacks that I would give my right arm to work with because they are good. Many of my partners in there are Chicanos and then there are whites that I can't stand either.

Part of the resentment over minorities involves promotions. Many white officers report a "reverse racism" whereby minorities seem to be promoted at a higher rate than white officers. A white officer reports:

It is funny, now I think there is more of a reverse discrimination than it used to be. . . . The black officers are very cliquish . . . I try to get along with everybody. But I don't go drinking with them. . . . There are some officers that I can make jokes with . . . we make racial jokes with each other but now racial jokes are very taboo in here—you can't call an inmate a greaser or a nigger . . . you can't call an officer that at all or it is five days [suspension] right there. . . . Inmates can call a white officer honkey or cracker but if you call that same inmate a nigger you are in trouble.

In describing the write-up for racial remarks, an old-time white officer says:

Some of the top administrators take the racial joking very seriously. They write up the white staff. There are very few black or Mexican staff who will receive any kind of disciplinary for making that kind of remark, but there are a great many black staff that seem to go out of their way to write up the white staff.

The opposite perspective on race relations is described by black officers. Among the male officers, race becomes the single defining issue. A black officer with experience in another prison says:

This race stuff really tripped me out. There have been some bad racial incidents among the officers . . . I was freaked out. This one black officer was out with a white female officer . . . and a sergeant lost his stripes over that because he acted a real fool and punched the black guy out. It was so bad that after that, the snack bar was segregated . . . black officers on one side and the white officers on the other . . . they were eye-balling each other. . . . The warden was pissed . . . he made an example of that. See the inmates love that stuff. They come up to you and say "Hey, did you hear what happened? . . . " They will tell you that some peckerwoods jumped an officer . . . and I took it with a grain of salt until I heard an officer tell me. It really shocked me because you would think that people in this area would be more tolerant.

Black officers who began work in the mid 1970s report difficulties in being among the first black officers in the pen. Several older black officers tell of harassment on the job, such as racist and annoying phone calls when occupying tower positions at night, or the questioning of their abilities as an officer and a man. The need to work together seems to be overridden by these racial divisions. One black officer points this out.

Yes, I think it [racism] is there, even more so than with the inmates. It is really terrible the way some officers treat other officers—you know, as officers, we have to depend on each other. . . . You could depend on me for your life someday and yet you treat me like scum . . . and I may need to help you when you really need it.

Many officers felt that racial segregation among the staff was encouraged by the previous administration but hope that the new regime will change this. A Chicano officer sees the tradition of racism as ending.

I think it is the structure . . . maybe there are still some problems in that area, but I don't think they are as bad as people have made them out to be . . . because I have seen a lot of good working relations. Good friendship . . . you know what that is? When you have to go in there and you have to go in a cell or you hear that whistle blow you only know two things— the green and the blue. And that is it, everything else goes by the wayside—at least it does now.

If it is a black inmate on a white inmate, the black officer on top of that black inmate and vice versa . . . it doesn't exist like it used to exist . . . and I mean I heard some really negative stuff at the academy. . . . I don't tolerate it . . . as a Mexican . . . I don't tolerate it from my fellow officers or . . . the inmates, . . . when you have to walk that tier, you depend on that guy.

A black female suggests that she was ignored by the white officers when she first came to work at San Quentin. She discovered that prisoners were a source of information.

There were no black officers on the yard, I was the only one. I talked to the black inmates and they trained me. They taught me how to watch my back, what to do if the alarm goes off in South Block. They even told me to stay on the yard with them if something happened inside. The white officers never talked to me. I had to be alone on the yard for eight hours because they ignored me. They said that I didn't do my job because I was talking to the inmates all the time.

Explicit racial conflicts occur over mixed marriages. White women officers, who have many obstacles, take on further difficulties when they are married to a nonwhite officer. Couples in this situation report harassment including telephone threats, destruction of their property, and harassment from prisoners as well as coworkers.

Gender

The introduction of women into the work force has had significant consequences for the worker's occupational culture. The presence of women in a very male world is unwelcome to most male workers. There is a sense that while minority males have been somewhat assimilated into this world, females are still facing obstacles. Zimmer (1986) describes these issues well. The objection to female workers at San Quentin found voice in the majority of the men interviewed. Where racial attitudes were couched in more subtle terms, opposition to female workers was direct. With few exceptions, the male sample declared that "women do not belong here." In response to this view, a highly respected woman officer commented, "When you get right down to it, no one really belongs there, but someone has to work there."

At the time of the study, women officers comprised about 20 percent of the front line. In the intensive interview sample, women were about 35 percent. Uniformly, these female respondents report a long period of being "tested," more by the officers than the prisoners, and continue to express uneasiness and unacceptance on the part of their male coworkers. This is a reflection of a gender-based perspective more than the actual work performance of the women officers. Most male officers will decry their female workers, but will also describe one "exception" to the negative image of female workers. When asked to give an example of a good worker, the majority of the sample listed women without qualifying their statements. Bob Powers offers this comment:

I have seen them [females] come and go. I personally don't think they should be here. For one thing, we have a no-hostage policy, if I was held, the warden would say, "Hey, we don't have hostages around here." I think that would be different for the women. If I saw three or four of these old arm-pushers [weight lifters] jumping on a woman and raping her, instead of blowing the whistle and getting out of the way, I would try to get those suckers off of her, not because she is an officer, but because she is female.

I don't think that men should work at CIW [California Institute for Women], if they want to be an employee of the CDC then they should work here. But they don't want to work down there. The inmates here will show some respect towards the female officers because they are female and then some of them around here can make me blush with their language. . . . Once she shows that side, she has dug her own grave, no one respects her.

I honestly don't think they should be here, but they are here and I can't keep them out. There are some females working here that I would rather have with me in a fight than some of these males. I think they would stand by me more than many of these men.

A traditional image of the female role is the root of some objections.

I don't think there is any reason for a woman to put herself into a potentially debasing and demeaning situation. There are positions that can be filled by women over there which wouldn't compromise a woman, but most of the positions that are there at San Quentin harden a woman, they detract from her femininity, her lifestyle, her vocabulary changes, even her dress style—her appearance. I don't think there's any place, except in certain selected positions. They're there so I'll have to live with it. There's a couple of them that do their job. They have the common sense and backed with experience that lets them perform their duties without fainting. The majority of women we have become hard and calloused, after two, three years, from exposure to San Quentin. They come to work, their vocabulary's clean . . . their walk, their whole mannerisms are feminine; two or three years later they sound like a stevedore. They walk like they've got a grudge against the world, taking it out on everybody and they lose their attractiveness.

Women workers are often put into a double bind by these ambivalent attitudes. On one hand, women are expected to "act like a man" and perform their duties. On the other hand, a woman may be openly criticized, by both men and women officers, as trying to act too much like a man. Among "accepted women," the most successful strategy seems to be to "act like yourself." Zimmer (1986) echoes this finding. This comment was made by most women officers when asked what kind of advice they would give a new female officer. Most of the longer term female officers feel that it is somewhat easier to start the job now that the institution has become used to the idea of female workers. One woman who currently holds a very prestigious job talks about being tested when she first started six years ago:

I knew that I was being watched by the other officers on the yard. I don't know that I could say that I was really tested out front, but I know that I was being watched all the time. If I talked to one inmate too much, they would start all kinds of rumors about you. I would come to work on time, stand out in the rain if I had to and I would never complain. One day, I just blew up at another officer. From that day on everything was cool . . . he would always tell me that I didn't belong on the yard and then one day I just blew up. I told him to never talk to me again unless he could talk to me with respect. He said, "What are you talking about?" and I said, "Don't you ever talk to me like that again, you motherfucker," and stormed out. I thought a big thing would come of it, but from that day on I was treated like royalty and I had no problems.

If you are a woman, they may throw you in a position that nobody wants where nobody wants you. You just have to be competent and then you will earn their respect.

A woman officer who is considering leaving the department says:

Deep down inside I am not sure that women should be working here. I don't think I personally like most of the other women. . . . When I am fifty years old, I can't see myself shaking down inmates or taking verbal abuse. But if things really got bad, like during a riot, a lot of the women can respond better than the men, the ones with the big stomachs. I think I would like to see women in better jobs, but I am there and I stay because the money is good.

SEXUAL POLITICS

An overall concern, expressed by men and women, is women who "promote on their backs." The male workers are concerned over the unfair advantage that women might have with the predominantly male administration. The women object because of the bad name it gives the whole sex. The concern that a woman can be promoted because of sexual favors with administrators has a second side, that of sexual harassment. A common reaction to a woman's promotion is: "It is not who you know, but who you blow." Women feel a double pressure in that sexual harassment makes their job harder and, at the same time, they spend considerable energy proving that they, themselves, are not "promoting on their back." Another key concern is the "macho" image of the correctional worker. One woman officer puts this threat well in perspective in saying:

Women bring about a calmer setting. It also forces the male officers not to act as "big, bad and tough" because here they have this little five foot two, 115 pound woman standing beside them, putting a guy that is six foot four, 230 pounds in cuffs . . . saying, "come on now, act right," and not having any problem doing it. Whereas he might have to go in there with two or three other guys and tackle him down to cuff him. It also forces them to recognize that they can't go home and talk about how bad and mean they are and what a tough day they have had because some little chickie can do the same thing that they're doing.

SEXUAL HARASSMENT

Many female officers report a steady amount of harassment from both the prisoners and the staff. The most common attitude was that "we expect it from the inmates, but we are disgusted at it from other officers." Sexual harassment by prison staff is generally not publicized. In the fall of 1981, the San Francisco Bay Area papers (Foote, 1981a) reported several cases of sexual harassment and noted that the problem came from an unexpected source, the workers rather than the prisoners.

During the present interviews, there were specific reports of offers for preferred days off or promotions in return for sexual favors. These respondents would very often mention the administrator by name. Recent attention by the unions to these problems has created some lawsuits to other institutions, although none were public at San Quentin at the time of the research. Female respondents were split on the question of sexual harassment. One woman who was married to an officer at another institution says:

I don't know about that [sexual politics] because I have never been approached. Maybe at the beginning when I first came here and nobody knew about my husband. Nobody approached me for nothing because of the way that I was—you have to be a certain kind of person for someone to ask you that anyway.

This traditional approach to the question of sexual harassment— that you have to be "that kind of person in order for it to happen to you"—can be shared by males and females. Some female officers, however, disagree with this point of view and see the problem as structural rather than personal. One female officer who has been working at the prison for many years says:

I tell you, all kinds [of men] used to hit on me, from the very top to the very bottom. I used to cry in the beginning because at that time I did not know that it could make me a rich woman (laughs). I had one top administrator breathing and panting on me, trying to touch my tits. Can you imagine? C.O.'s will ask you out for dinner or a drink, or for my phone number. Some man even came up to me and said, "I would sure like to have sex with you."

Another woman sees the acts of sexual harassment as an extension of the way in which women were constantly tested by the other officers:

You really have to prove yourself in there, prove yourself as a good cop. You have to show that you can be one of the boys and still be a woman. It is a dual role. You get ribbed a lot . . . like, "Can you really use that gun?" A lot of the sexual crap. I have not really been propositioned yet, but I am sure I will because everybody tells me that. I'd like to get that on tape—a proposition from a superior officer! I'd take it right to the top. It is so macho in there, they will take you out for a drink and say they fucked you even if they didn't . . . I heard about myself and I should know, right? I heard that I am a sure thing if you take me out for a drink. . . . They will slanderize you at every opportunity if they can. The gossip is vicious.

Informal sexual harassment is harder to deal with than the formal. An often repeated story tells of a male officer who had a relationship with a female officer and after the relationship was over, the male would show nude pictures of the woman to both staff and prisoners. Another story tells of a male officer who spread stories ("she has crabs") about a woman officer who refused to have a physical relationship. In the small town of the prison community, these incidents become common knowledge. As a result, women may refuse to become involved with male officers or insist on keeping these relationships a secret. Not until the relationship has been formally sanctioned by engagement or marriage do most women let others know of their involvement. Relationships among the correctional workers are not uncommon, but the courtship period is often kept quiet.

A hard-line approach to the sexual issues was taken by a male officer who argues that women should not be allowed to work in the prison because, "Some of them go to bed with the inmates. I think the lesbian officers get along best because they are not influenced by a nice body that a convict might have." Women are also seen as potential sexual partners for officers as this passage illustrates.

When the officers get together and get drunk, all they talk about is how it is on the job, about all the women they want to screw on the job, that is what guys do, they are crazy. [*But don't men everywhere do that?*] Yes, but there it is different . . . to those convicts the women working there are the only ones that they ever see. . . . A woman goes to work there and gets more attention than she ever had in her life . . . it is unbelievable—it must rub off on them [workers] because they get to thinking women officers are the only women in the world, too. . . . There are some officers who say, as soon as a new female walks in, "I am going to get that; I am going to take that." I just tell them to go to a disco or a bar, but I understand because when I was at Soledad I thought that too, and that the only place I could meet a woman was on the job.

Even among the women, conflicts over sexual issues emerge. A black woman who has been employed for five years tells of her experiences with this system.

When I first started, there was this older woman who really knew about life and took me under her wing, but then after six months our friendship broke up. I really admired her and then she stopped speaking to me. It really hurt me and finally I asked her why . . . we were in front of Four Post at that time and it was packed. . . . I whispered to her, "Why are you not speaking to me?" and she told me that it was because I had been fucking Sergeant so-and-so . . . which was ridiculous because I saw him as a father figure and he had never even made a pass at me. . . . He just liked me and respected me and I found out that everybody assumed we had something going because he took me under his wing. He looked after me because he saw that everyone else was playing games on me, the staff and the inmates, and he offered me a job in the kitchen and I took it to get off the yard. . . .

So I said to her, "You think I am fucking Sergeant so-and-so?" and she said, "Yes," . . . so I really went off on her and told her that it was none of her business and that I did not owe her an explanation about my life. I just told her like it was and then I told the sergeant and he said that he had heard it too, and that I should not worry about it. And that was the just the beginning of all that stuff.

This example illustrates how the power of rumor not only separates women and men officers, but serves to divide women officers from productive relationships with each other. The power of rumor and suspicion eliminates any worker solidarity and fuels the intense competition for scarce rewards among the officers. Rumors are a significant source of conflict and social control among the workers. The power of the prison grapevine among prisoners is well documented and this process extends to the correctional officer community. A seasoned black officer says:

Staff is always the problem here. If we just had to come and deal with the inmates, life would be beautiful. But here you have to come to work and worry about being stabbed in the back by a staff member. The rumors and the lies that can be put out about you are tremendously powerful. If you are late, for example, somebody will put a jacket on you for being late all the time . . . all kinds of different things. If we did not have anything to worry about but inmates, this would be an easy job.

See you really have control over the inmates and they really can't bother you. The only time an inmate bothers you is if you are an asshole or if he does not know you. The inmates are really good about putting the word out. "Hey, there is a guy that you don't mess with." There are lots of inmates that I don't even know that come up to me and say, "Hey, Officer D_____ . . . how are you doing? . . . " and they understand that you may not know who he is, but he knows who you are. If somebody greets you, you answer.

The impact of rumor is tied to the informal distribution of power that is recognized by all those familiar with the real hierarchy of the prison. Although everyone interviewed recognized the danger of rumors, most accepted their existence and described their participation in them. One new woman officer said, quite simply, "They are awful, but they are fun." The absence of any formal communication network among the officers as a group, the existence of the informal power arrangements, and the inability to predict the rise and fall of one's personal fortunes provide a solid framework for the workings of the rumors. As one's reputation and credibility are the most useful resource possessed by the officer, every worker is susceptible to the negative impact of rumors.

Rumors fall into four general categories. For women, an additional category of sexual involvements (with prisoners, staff, and administrators) exists. The general rumor categories are:

1. Power (being in the car, out of favor)
2. Job competence (being incompetent, being trustworthy, a PC [Protective Custody] officer)
3. Involvement with prisoners (being "dirty," being fair)
4. General character (being an alcoholic, happily married, being respected, being weak, or racial/gender issues)

These overlapping categories of rumor can directly affect one's reputation and one's informal working relationships. Because of the nature of the work and the intense turnover rate, few officers have the opportunity to interact with the same officer on a daily basis. An individual officer may not be "known" through face-to-face interaction, but may have a jacket through the grapevine that may or may not be based on actual fact. A white, male officer still on probation describes a situation whereby an older officer "played a trick on him," setting the scene for the probationary worker to look foolish in front of a group of officers and prisoners. Although the second officer publicly admitted that the scene was a set-up and not the fault of the probationary worker, the new officer's reputation was damaged. This new officer recognized the power of the rumor and that the actual circumstances of the story would never be known, only the fact that he had made a foolish mistake.

This officer sadly, but correctly, concluded that the damage to his reputation was insurmountable.

The importance of the reputation is enlarged by its fragile nature. In a world founded on an informal power structure, a lack of significant interaction among officers and across the official hierarchy and informed by a significant and intimidating tradition, the rumor emerges as a powerful device which can shape one's reputation. The relationship between rumor and power is significant. Those most likely to be affected by rumor are those who do not enjoy the advantages of juice, or a secure reputation. For those with San Quentin savvy, rumors can be used as a mechanism to reproduce and sustain the existing power relations by discrediting those who are powerless under the existing order.

IMAGES OF PRISONERS

Another conflict among officers concerns the definitions of prisoners. This is primarily related to how long one has worked inside the system, but can also be correlated with education, personal background, and specific types of experiences with prisoners. The wide majority of old-timers repeat the phrase: "We don't have trouble with inmates, we have trouble with the staff or the administration." New employees have an ambiguous approach to the prisoners. Those with some college education state that they see prisoners as "people who need help," or people who should be accorded a minimum set of rights as guaranteed by law. However, the image of the prisoner as a dangerous villain is reinforced consistently by the training, the war stories, and many times by the actual experience of working in a maximum security institution. The changing characteristics of the population give more reason for the old-timers to talk of the "good old days." As the population changes from seasoned old-timers to younger prisoners and less experienced workers, the changes in the culture have a significant effect on the image of prisoners held by the officers.

Few "old-timers" seemed interested in the nature of the crime of conviction, but a majority of those very new to the job expressed a concerted interest. Probationary employees were particularly concerned with the specifics of the prisoners' criminal histories. One female worker still on probation felt quite strongly that "it is my right to know if I am working in an area with convicted rapists." Such concern, again, is not part of the general worldview of the older officers who rarely inquire about the nature of the crime. The group of seasoned workers tends to dismiss the newer workers' concern as "fear of the prisoners." Many stories are told of officers who are "afraid of their own shadow, much less a convict."

This disagreement as to the nature of the prisoners is translated into conflicts over defining the nature of the job. This conflict separates workers who have the same job title and may even work in similar positions. On one hand, older officers speak of not being able to trust the training and the perspective of the newcomers. On the other, the newer workers see the older workers as nonprofessional and perceive them to be unemployable in any other setting. These conflicts, rooted in the length of service and the developing definition of the role of the worker, continue to divide the workers.

THE ELITE

Cliques are central to the informal hierarchy of the prison worker. These cliques have substantive ties to the formal power structure and the less formal alliances among groups of workers. The existence of a powerful group of "insiders" was suggested by all respondents. The majority of officers feel "left out" of policy making and feel that they have very little control over their overall position in the institution. These cliques were described as "the inner circle" by the majority of those interviewed. Few officers suggested that they had some connection with these insiders. Of those who indicated some connection, the general feeling was that others saw them as having this special access to power, or "juice." When interviewed, those named did not feel they had any special claim to power beyond that of an ordinary line officer.

The claim to membership in the elite can be through formal,

recognized positions, or through an informal acknowledgment of juice. A job assignment on the yard or with the special security squad (commonly known as "gooners" among the prisoners) signifies upward mobility and an elite status among the rest of the guards. One former yard officer says:

The yard officers used to be the elite, everyone knew that they knew their jobs and were next in line for the promotions. We even had our own stance, it was somewhat of a joke, but it worked. You lean against the wall, and act like you are not paying attention (illustrates stance). I have a friend who made a lot of busts that way and now he is a sergeant.

The special security squad is another highly desirable position with status. At San Quentin, the squad wears a jumpsuit uniform, with combat boots and other military hardware. Until very recently, squad membership was informally closed to female officers, except for office positions of keeping records on gang members. Several women have since won permanent positions on the squad and roam the prison in search of contraband and investigating any suspected gang activity. One female squad member recognizes the relative authority held by the squad in her remarks given to new officers:

Most of you will see us as a cut above the rest of the officers and in a way that is true, but you have to remember that this is your institution, not just ours', and we are only as good as you can make us. We all have to work together, and if you find that you can't, get out.

The squad also illustrates the image of the "super cop," one that most officers try to discourage because it does not facilitate teamwork among workers. A male squad member takes exception to this advice and says:

Most of you will hear things about being a super cop, and I want to tell you that this has positive and negative sides of it. Even when I was on the line, I was criticized for being an overachiever, a go-getter, for outperforming everybody else in my unit. Well, that was me, and that is one of the reasons that I am on the squad.

Here is an open acknowledgment of the competition for the few scarce rewards, such as promotions and status, available to the officers. Being a "cut above" is offered as a reward for those who "out perform" others.

OLD TIMERS VS. YOUNGSTERS: A GENERATION GAP

Although racial and gender discrimination continues, the most serious conflict among the line staff concerns older, more experienced officers and the large number of new recruits. The high turnover rate of the front-line officer creates a serious worker shortage with a range of consequences. At the time of the study, over 80 percent of those working as correctional officers have been with the prison for less than one year. So much of the job depends on "common sense," a specific kind of knowledge about the prison which is grounded in day-to-day experience. Many of the old-time officers (now defined as anyone with more than four or five years at San Quentin) express a concern over the abilities of those newly hired. In some instances, this concern takes the form of questioning their abilities and may be couched in terms of race or gender. The overwhelming concern, however, lies with the abilities of the new officers to look out for themselves and to keep the prison functioning from day to day. Resentment is expressed against those "youngsters" who do not fit individualized perceptions of what the job entails, or what makes a good officer. One veteran of eight years, when asked what makes a good officer, replied, "One who works like I do." This is essentially a conflict between worldviews which presents opposing definitions of prisoners, other staff, and the role of the correctional worker. These conflicting worldviews also present conflicting relationships with issues of power and material interests.

Being new on the job has never been easy. New officers report being ignored by other officers until the newly hired officer has proven himself under a variety of circumstances. The huge influx of new workers has made inexperience the norm and has confirmed the suspicions of old-timers. The conflict between the two groups—old-timers and youngsters—is recognized by all members of the prison community. In 1982, an editorial in the *San Quentin News*, the prisoner newspaper, described the emerging conflicts between old-time San Quentin workers and prisoners and the new wave of young, inexperienced officers and the "new breed" of prisoners entering the system. This article acknowledged the common culture carried by both workers and prisoners who have "done time" at San Quentin. Ways in which those new to the prison did not understand the tradition and folkways specific to San Quentin culture were also discussed. The supposed adversarial relationship between the blue (prisoner) and the green (worker) disappears, to be replaced by a unique "generation gap" between youngsters and old-timers. A nostalgia for the "good old days" when cops and convicts understood each other was expressed by many of the old-time officers. True, much of this understanding was based on coercion and a lack of specified rights of the prisoners, but most of the "old-time" workers talk about the old days in positive terms.

McCoy (1981, p. 178) describes a conflict in style between old and new workers:

Unfortunately, Parley sighed, too many guards did not have their wits about them. "In front of convicts, I've had to personally go up to a fish officer [rookie guard] and tell him to shut his goddamn mouth. The confrontation this officer was creating because of ignorance was a bum beef on the convict and was going to cause a big scene."

A young sergeant who was determined to make a career of corrections said that the situation was further aggravated by the lack of communication between the new guards and the veterans. The new guards drew the tough assignments in the cellblocks or in the yard, he said, while the old-timers waited out their pensions at desk or tower jobs removed from hostile inmates. "An 'old school' lieutenant sits at his desk and tells a fish cop to go down there and tell some convicts to do something," the young sergeant grumbled, "and the convicts laugh at him."

Even those officers who qualify for old-timer status talk about being tested when they first started, but expressed desire to help with new officers. A female officer with six years experience says:

[When I first started] the officers would not tell me what to do; your job description never really tells you anything, just when to report to work and when to leave. I really did not know what to do. I felt awkward standing on the yard and the only time I knew what to do was when I was escorting someone and the inmate would tell me where to go. . . . I did not know what to do if someone got stabbed, except to blow my whistle, and that was about it. I think they don't tell you much of the time because they do not know themselves and then you always hear the old-timers say, "Let them learn like I did—the hard way!" whatever that means. . . . I feel that, starting at San Quentin when I did, they wanted me to fall flat on my face so I could get fired. It is a little better now. I have seen people come and go, and I will pull them over to the side and introduce myself. I have a real big heart and I always want to be the good guy. Hi, my name is A———, and if you need any help I am here, and I can tell them what they have to do and what they have to watch out for and they just look at you like you have shit on them or something.

They say, "I don't need you to tell me anything"—very seldom do you get anybody that will accept what you tell them . . . [the attitude is] hey, I know what is going on here. But this is my sixth year here, and I still don't know what this place is all about. Things constantly change here, and these new people have that really negative attitude.

The assertion that all the new officers don't want advice was not borne out in the few interviews with officers on probation. A white, male officer with several years as a police officer, but only six months at the prison, says:

I don't think most of the older officers there are all that professional— that is how I see my job. It is frustrating for those of us who want to change things. A lot of the older ones should probably be delivering mail—they would still have their security. I personally have not seen these good officers that everyone talks about. They have gone elsewhere— to outside patrol, Four Post, the towers. They are not on the ground or they are in the hospital. Where are they when we need them?

This animosity between the older and younger officers is partially grounded in the competition for promotions and other rewards. On one hand, old-timers may have an advantage in obtaining desired promotions. (A recent contract by the union introduces seniority as a determining factor for many rewards. This contract, however, does not solve the problems of competition of their informal rewards. Other states, such as New York, use seniority as the primary basis for promotion or positions.) On the other hand, the older workers see those with much less experience promoting very quickly and leaving them behind. Whether the lack of promotions is due to politics, "juice," or actual competence is hard to determine. Old-timers strongly feel that they have been left behind and see the "younger generation" as obtaining the promotions, good positions, and rewards that they feel should be rightfully theirs. This bitterness shapes their attitude toward other workers (the majority of whom are youngsters), the administration, and the system as a whole. These resentments cause the older workers to opt for positions "off the ground" and to stay in the towers for their remaining years. Many studies of correctional workers have misinterpreted the motivation for this trend by saying that older officers are fed up with the prisoners, and that they seek these noncontact positions as an escape from the prisoners. Time and time again, old-timers counter this explanation by saying, "Hell no, we don't have trouble with most of the convicts. If all I had to do was deal with convicts all day, my job would be a snap." Antagonistic relations among the workers appear to be a much greater problem.

One black officer with several years of experience in the system has decided to avoid the competition and take a relief position that is undesirable except for the fact that no one will try to take it from him.

Nobody will talk bad about me to try and get it. Nobody wants the days off. Wednesdays and Thursdays. When you have Saturday and Sunday, all kinds of people will stab you in the back. There is a lot of gossip. You will have the inmates come and tell you when other officers are talking about you. Of course, you have to take it with a grain of salt as you consider the source. But the inmates like to see us fight among ourselves, to get so mad at each other that we don't help each other so they can go and do what they want.

Avoiding the competition for jobs and rewards is one way of avoiding conflict with other officers, but several alternate dimensions of struggle exist. Security risks, dependability, and overall trust rank as the second highest area of concern expressed in the interviews. In a maximum security prison most of the actual security is provided by the gun rail positions. Officers on the ground, or in close contact with the prisoners, do not carry weapons and must depend on those in the gun positions to insure their safety. This becomes a highly controversial area because many officers no longer feel they can depend on the gun coverage for their personal safety. Often voiced about women officers (who "only passed because of personal attention on the gun range"), most officers worry that those in the gun rail positions do not know what they are doing. A female worker tells of the time she went to relieve another female, a newcomer, from a gun tower position and discovered that this officer had held a live round in the gun and did not know how to remove it. Another female officer tells of being relieved by a male officer new to the job who asked her how he could tell the convicts from the officers. This individual was so new that he had not been told of the basic difference in clothes that separate the two (prisoners in blue, officers in green and tan). She stayed late, on her own time, to explain to him the differences "even though some of the officers look as scroungy as the inmates." She left, telling him to call his sergeant if he was not sure what to do. In the interview, she commented, "This really hurt me to see this happen, and I am supposed to depend on these people for my safety?"

Another central conflict occurs over informal policy changes. While the director's rule book is designed to set policy in a general way, the immediate supervisors, generally a sergeant or a lieutenant, set the routine for the unit. Although some units have organized meetings to set these policies and to convey the days' events to the incoming shift, this was somewhat unusual at the time of the interviews. (Follow-up observations suggest that this policy is becoming more widespread.) One officer remembers that the idea of a meeting was very foreign to others outside the unit because most people had gotten used to the piecemeal approach to policy in the unit. The discretion of the individual officer is both a positive and a negative aspect of the job. Having the authority to make a decision on the spot is a key contradiction of the job, but many times these decisions are overridden by a superior officer. This is a particular source of resentment when an officer attempts to discipline a prisoner and her action is overridden by a sergeant. Writing a 115, a formal disciplinary report which can result in loss of privileges, is one way an officer can discipline a prisoner. Many times 115's are thrown out as insignificant and impractical. One high-ranking officer has commented that "writing a 115 shows me that the officer has failed and lost control over the situation." This procedure leaves the officer feeling powerless and causes the prisoner to feel like he has "beat" the officer.

ATTITUDES TOWARD BRUTALITY

Most officers report the existence of brutality, but few offer any firsthand knowledge of it. Martin Sobell, who did federal time for alleged involvement in the Rosenberg conspiracy case, comments on prison brutality:

There was little overt brutality at Alcatraz, certainly less than at the other penitentiaries. The small population made it dangerous for the guards to be cruel to the men, because brutality was more difficult to conceal and word got around more quickly. But the cruelty of the whole institution exceeded any possible individual cruelties on the part of the guards (Sobell, 1974, p. 400).

A small minority of those interviewed admit to participating in physical abuse of prisoners, but describe the violence in terms of the specific situation and the frustration of the workers built up over a long time. There was no evidence of any systematic efforts at brutality and most reports of violence were isolated incidents. The general consensus in the interviews was that most officers do not like to see violence, if only because it makes their job harder in the long run.

The following remarks were most typical of the responses to the question of violence.

I have not seen it, but I have heard about it. I have had many officers come to me and say that they have seen other officers go off, kick a guy or beat him with a baton while they were handcuffed, and they all want to know what to do. That really is a difficult question to me because I really feel that there is nobody around that I could trust. Other people have seen it happen, but I have not. I don't know what I would do, but I would never participate in it. I think it has to be frustrated officers, or some of these racist officers.

Another officer, a black male with several years on the force, says:

Well, it doesn't happen much anymore, not like it used to be . . . because prisons used to run themselves. Now that the courts run the prisons a little bit, you have to let up on them. You used to beat guys up all the time. Not too much. Sure, I've seen it. One time I didn't participate in this because it really made me mad . . . they beat one dude up and a sergeant came all the way from the South Block. He ran about sixty yards: there is about five cops in there, and he came over and started kicking the dude. I did nothing when I saw that . . . I stood there. I was angry, but you can't say anything because if you say something, they aren't going to stop just because you say something. Too, if you say something, they put you on the opposite end and say stuff like, " . . . you got to watch him, he is friends with the convicts." One of the worse things you can be there, because then they are on you all the time. . . . They feel like you're packing or doing something illegal. I don't mess around with that shit. I'm there for the money. It is just a job for me. I like to go in there and do my job and come home and live my life. . . . I know it is best not to force my opinion. I don't think a lot of the officers who participated in it—not when they do it that way. It would all depend on the situation . . . if he tries to stick a cop that is one thing . . . it makes you mad if someone hits you.

The use of unnecessary force is a central issue for the prison administration who has taken steps to stop violence. With this policy the number of officers who object to violence on principle and brutality against prisoners appears to have increased significantly. The informal sanctions and the threat of being reported seems to be the greatest determining factor. These processes have combined to create an atmosphere that discourages brute force in all but the most extreme or individualized incidents.

Still, the possibility of violence is always there. A relatively new officer comments:

I have never seen it, but I believe that it could happen. Officers are continually harassed, and they let it build up. There is no opportunity to let off all that anger physically. Although I think some of the officers definitely would [be violent] if they could.

One officer who "would if he could" takes this direct position on the use of violence.

It goes with the job. It always depends on how the inmates act, if you ask them not to move and they move, then "their ass is ours," whether it is necessary or not. If they don't do what you ask, if they won't come up to the bars, then you have to go after them. I have seen tear gas overused, and I don't think that was right.

Bowker (1980, p. 102) describes brutality against prisoners as conditions beyond those "imposed upon the prisoners by the official institutional policies and the state." Such a statement subjectively defines brutality as that which exceeds acceptable limits. Overall, Bowker suggests physical brutality against prisoners appears to be decreasing, even in southern prisons where systematic abuse has been clearly documented. Toch (1977) sees that violence against prisoners is a part of the subcultural norms that favor this violence. He found that brutality often takes the form of choke-holds used to restrain prisoners. In general, he suggests that these norms arise out of workers' fears of prisoners and are part of the "trench warfare climate" of the prison.

CONCLUSION

These conflicts, both structural and personal, shape relations among coworkers. Whether grounded in traditions of the prison, or created through situational events, these conflicts divide the prison work force. Race and sex are examples of traditional division. Situational conflicts are related to divergent definitions of the situation, of the role, and often of the prison itself. These conflicts, and their resolutions, contribute significantly to the worldview of the correctional worker.

For the worker, social control has both structural and situational origins. The formal social order of the prison places specific formal social controls on one's activities. On the surface, these rules appear necessary to the maintenance of order within the institution. Beyond this maintenance function, the normative structure of the prison dictates rule-bound behavior as it flows through the prison hierarchy. This social control is parallel to both formal and informal power. "Juice" is a property of workers and prisoners, and may be obtained through long-term friendships or association with those in power, or by occupying a pivotal position in the prison. Power, in whatever form, may be intangible but its role in the reproduction of social control shapes the delivery of this control on workers as well as prisoners.

5
Toward a New Typology

WORKER SUBCULTURES

Constructing a workable definition of the situation is the central problem for the correctional worker. One frequently cited solution is the worker subculture (Duffee, 1974; Esselstyn, 1966; Blum, 1976; Johnson and Price, 1981; Crouch and Marquart, 1981; Cheatwood, 1974; and Lombardo, 1981a). The notion of a worker subculture is parallel to that of a police subculture (Bordua, 1967; Skolnick, 1962; and Wambaugh, 1972). An early study of prison workers (Esselstyn, 1966) applies the concept of the officer subculture and describes a "technical language" which both communicates and maintains important cultural boundaries.

The technical language of corrections enters into the way and the circumstances in which correctional workers interact with each other. It is highly specialized and largely unintelligible to outsiders; its use promotes unity among those who understand it.

The exceedingly complex technical language of corrections includes rich mixtures from the law, medicine and the social and behavioral sciences. It includes terms from prison argot, the underworld and street corner slang.

It serves the same functions as do all secret languages—fencing out the stranger, speeding the transmission of ideas, and above all, strengthening one's life purpose and the friendly responses which it evokes, re-enforcing one's self-worth (Esselstyn, 1966, p. 79).

Toch and Klofas (1981) argue that the officer world is not characterized by these common bonds, but rather by a misunderstanding called "pluralistic ignorance." Pluralistic ignorance is a concern with public opinion, and the development of a perspective grounded "not in what I think but in what I think others think" (Toch and Klofas, 1982, p. 6). Cheatwood (1974) sees that the worker is a man caught in the middle of two organizational cultures. The culture of the staff, he suggests, is "produced in the interplay between interpersonal interaction with the inmate culture and their formal occupational relations with the administration" (p. 178). Chang and Zastrow (1976) argue that the workers do manifest group solidarity and that the opposition with the inmates produces an "us versus them" version of the world. This solidarity is grounded in the antagonism that workers feel from prisoners. Prigmore and Watkins (1972) suggest that the worker occupies an "equally captive world" as they live side by side with prisoners. E. H Johnson (1981) suggests that the worker culture is informed by private interests and individual personalities which are mediated by fixed ways of relating in the social structure.

Duffee (1974, p. 91) sees that the officer subculture "is born of the frustrating belief that inmates on the whole, deserve better treatment than the officers (or others) are capable of giving under the present circumstance." While studies of organizational cultures are central to understanding institutional life (Martin, 1983), the structural conflicts of the prison provide little evidence of a single subculture. Toch and Klofas (1982) found five basic types among their sample: the discouraged subculturalist, the supported majority, the lonely brave, the subcultural custodians, and the subcultural consensus estimators. The following discussion suggests a different approach, based on career stages and work styles based on the relations of the shop floor.

As described above, social interaction among officers is subtly negotiated. The conflicts of the shop floor can translate into strained relations among these workers. Distrust and suspicion, grounded in the basic competition for power and other rewards, may create a barrier between officers that is only overcome by contact which erodes negative relations. Frequency of interaction over time was the most common way of developing relationships, but an intense experience, brought on by a crisis or emergency also had the effect of creating these lasting relationships. Most of the distrust about other officers was grounded in a lack of personal knowledge about the coworker. If an officer could see that others were dependable, either on a day-to-day basis or in an emergency, initial barriers were broken down. Most officers report they only trust other officers whom they have known for a long time or with whom they have gone through "the wars."

In dangerous situations, such as a riot, workers are forced to transcend their differences and act as one. The line between workers and prisoners is most clear in a crisis. Workers look out for the safety of others and present a united front, both during the event and in its retelling. At San Quentin, the retelling of a story can be as important as the event itself. This type of emergency situation can create bonds of solidarity among workers. But a crisis does not automatically generate solidarity. Divisions among workers can be maintained, if not aggravated, during critical events.

Many times officers are not sure of the motives and goals of the other workers and this creates misunderstandings and the varying definitions of situations which cause the barriers between the officers. The comment "he doesn't know what he is doing," or "she doesn't have any common sense," is in fact a statement of the divergent definitions of the situation each actor brings to bear on the shop floor. For example, if one officer feels another officer is acting out of pure self-interest, rather than out of the interests of the whole, the first officer is most likely to stereotype the behavior of the second officer in terms of self-interest. In this working environment self-interest is defined as exclusive of the group interest and thereby perceived as a threat.

Lack of control over one's work characterizes the position of the correctional worker. Over time, most old-timers accept the nature of the work and develop personalized ways of gathering some influence over their work day. The most successful mechanisms involve the development of an attitude toward the job which defines their role in a specific, professional, and limited way. Working out relations with prisoners and with one's coworkers in the most constructive way is the primary method through which most old-timers come to accept their job and, in their words, "make the best of a bad situation." These resolutions of the conflicts presented by the unequal distribution of power and the structural working conditions of the prison shape the range of approaches and "types" of workers.

A TYPOLOGY OF WORKERS

These typologies are drawn from workers' descriptions of their own management strategies and their versions of approaches used by fellow workers. These descriptions are authentic in the sense that they are drawn directly from subjective experience rather than from observations made by a nonparticipant in this world. The first dimension ranges from a positive to a negative assessment of others in terms of a continuum of "weak" to "respected." The second dimension dovetails with the first in terms of the officer's relationship to power relations, treatment of prisoners, "macho behavior," approaches to the rules, and overall adjustment to the authority inherent in the job.

Two basic perspectives exist on the question of "types." Some officers see this question in terms of stages or processes that an officer goes through. This can be described as a "natural history" of approaches to the jobs. Some of these descriptions were directly tied to institutional and structural changes, based on changes in the administration or in the "mission" of the current central administration. Others saw officers in terms of types that described their approach to the job and detailed the relations with power, prisoners, and other workers.

The occupational culture of the correctional worker becomes part of the individual worldview through socialization. The worker, in turn, contributes to this social order through actions and meanings. In Giddens's (1979) terms, this is the process of the production and reproduction of social life. In describing the ways in which an officer comes to make sense of the new prison world, these types also illustrate the production and maintenance of social control.

A NATURAL HISTORY OF THE JOB

Several officers explained the process of obtaining the culture of the worker through a three-stage process. The first step of this process is characterized by "going by the book" and being very official in all dealings. One officer describes it this way:

Usually you go through what I call the professional period when you first start . . . you are scared of being fired, because you are still on probation, you go exactly by the book even when it does not make sense. You are not sure of your own authority and you hide behind the book, right down the line. If someone, anyone, tries to usurp your authority, you get scared and you don't know how to act, so you go super-professional. You get out of it and you gain self-confidence through experience and then you get into the badge heavy thing.

"Going by the book" is judged as naive by the majority of old-timers. The gaps between official policy and the attempts at getting through the day are personified in the new officer. Older workers smile at the new officers' attempts to make sense of the complicated prison culture by using the book, and are often willing to let the newcomers "find out for themselves" what the job "actually means." The "actual" meaning of the work is highly individualized and mediated by one's relationship with the power structure of the prison. This combination of background, on the job experiences, and relationship to the power structure (for example, having juice, being in or out of favor) determines the emergent approaches to the job.

Coming out of this neophyte period is contingent on contact with other officers and with prisoners. During the second period the new worker solidifies his relationships with the prison order. Very often, the worker does not reconcile the conflicts of the shop floor. He may not develop a workable way of solving problems with prisoners. In this period, officially circumscribed by a "probationary" period (but which actually extends much longer), an officer decides whether this reconciliation is possible or even worth the effort. The inability to reconcile the structural and personal conflicts which characterize the work account for the extremely high turnover rate of the correctional worker. Much has been made of the conflicts with prisoners the worker experiences and the first cut at explaining this turnover rate is cast as an "inability to work with prisoners." Further examination of the life round of the correctional worker and the day-to-day routine of the job suggests that working with prisoners is only a small part of the problems of the job.

The structural and institutional contradictions as well as the personalized conflicts with one's coworkers intensely affect the worker, more seriously than the solvable problems of working with prisoners. The second career stage involves attempts at reconciling such conflicts. Becoming "badge heavy" is one attempt at this reconciliation. Badge heavy is a street police term which accurately captures the perspective and behavior of becoming immersed in only part of the prison culture. Other terms used to explain this hyper-concern with one's authority include "super cop," macho (used on both men and women workers), power tripping, John Wayne type, wanting points, and "wannabees." (Wannabee is originally a street term which describes a young street kid who "wants to be" a gang member, usually distinguished by a pattern of dress or speech, but is not part of the gang. Wannabee signifies a desire "to be," but at the same time a sense that this person will never really make it to that goal.) Most officers admit to having been through this stage in one form or another. The danger and the futility of "being on a power trip" within an institution grounded in negotiated relations was also recognized. Being "badge heavy" can jeopardize one's personal safety and the safety of others as the following incident illustrates.

One day I was chased with a knife and that really scared me and [made me realize] that I was feeling badge heavy that day—being super [thinking] I am invincible. When you are badge heavy, this badge feels this big and [you think] that it can protect you from anything. . . . We had a stabbing on one side of East Block—and I was going to catch the guys as they were coming around.

I was not thinking . . . I didn't even look to see where the gun man was or any others were, it was stupid because I was not thinking. I was only thinking about the glory and everything else. I was going to be tough so I ran around this corner and there was this guy with a knife, he had blood all over him because he had stabbed that guy. He looked at me and I looked at him and he saw that nobody else was around. . . . And then I looked around and that was it, I turned around and left and he came after me. He started after me, and you can paint me a coward if you want to, but I ran and he chased me. Luckily enough another officer showed up and the gun man responded to the situation. He saw what was happening and cracked one off. The guy threw the knife in a cell and tried to fade into the woodwork. I ran into the other officers but I was scared shitless and everything else, but then I went back up there with the other officers and the guy was still there, said "Watch him, he has a knife." We snatched him up and pinned the murder on him, an attempted assault on staff, we got the weapon and it was a good case. It turned out good but it was the stupidest thing I have ever done. Never again will I do something like that. When you begin to feel badge heavy, usually after two or three years, everything goes to your head. Every cop goes through that—they feel the authority, it is basically a life or death authority over the inmates. Most people come out of it but some of them don't.

Whether a permanent perspective, or just a rite of passage, the phenomenon of being a super cop is dangerous to prisoners and other workers as well. Being on the "macho" trip, and feeling the power generated by the norms of the coercive institution does not restrict itself to male officers. The female who acts in a "macho" way also comes under criticism.

I remember one day I was on the upper yard, an officer had stopped an inmate to shake him down. I was standing behind them and a third officer, female, stopped as she was walking by when he said "hands on the wall," she yelled "up against the wall" so loudly that everyone turned around. They are just trying to prove that the inmates don't scare them. But it is not necessary. I don't have to struggle with someone because the gun coverage is there to protect us.

The issue of authority is not fully reconciled at this stage. Being in charge can color the worldview in such a way that many workers carry this perspective out the gates into their home lives. Several officers told stories of ordering their wives and children around when they got off the job. One wife finally told her husband that he would have to change because "you are treating us like those inmates you have in there. We are not in prison, even though you seem to think so."

The third stage for those officers who remain at San Quentin, and who do not promote and transfer is characterized as the "old-timer" phase.

You know what is going on, you have the experience to know every kind of inmate there is and you are able to differentiate among those types and you know how to deal with individuals, both staff and inmates. You know the physical layout—every hiding hole, places where inmates hide things, and places where officers hide out. You just know what is going on and that takes a lot of time.

In short, this last stage is related to the development of the "common sense" which is essential to getting through the day. The unique aspect of this "common sense" is that it is not common to anyone walking in off the street, but a very specific translation of experience grounded in the prison culture. It is only "common" in the sense that it is shared by those with similar tenure and experience as correctional workers, and a similar relationship to the structure of the prison.

Although these stages are represented as process, static ideal types emerge from them. These types span a continuum from "good officer" to "weak officer" with those "just doing their eight hours" in the middle. It must be noted here that officers rarely belong in one single category, over time as well as from day to day. Although a general orientation can be derived from the three stages listed above, the core of these types lies in interaction and relations, and as such, becomes subjected to situational interplay. The officer who is consistent, however, is held in great regard: "If you are going to be a good guy, be a good guy; if you are going to be an asshole, be an asshole. But don't change up."

A female probationary employee describes her reaction to the notion of consistency.

I don't understand this term consistency. They stress it all the time in the academy—firm, fair, and consistent. But how can you be consistent when an inmate is cool with you one minute and calling you a bitch and telling you he's going to fuck you in the ass the next. And that is how it goes. How can you be consistent when one day you are working a shift—only eight hours—and you have had lots of sleep. The next time you work that shift you have worked three doubles since then, and you are exhausted and fed up. And hung over. I am not saying that one day you are cool and the next day you are an asshole. But we have moods, you can't get rid of them. There are times when I want to say, "Hey fuck you guys, get out of my face" when an hour before that I would not have been like that, but something will happen, like I'll get in a verbal confrontation with an inmate and that will blow my mood for the day.

Given the fluid nature of the types, the general dimensions of officer types follows. Again, respect and weakness are cornerstones to these definitions.

Respect

Respect is a fundamental value for both prisoners and workers. While specific to the prison, the notion of respect carries over to the everyday meanings. "Showing respect" in the prison is the ultimate in civilized behavior, "fronting someone off" is its opposite. Respect translates to treating each person as an individual, without any attempt to scam them, or be dishonest in any way. The most respected people in the pen, whether workers or prisoners, are those who maintain a consistent demeanor, who stand by their word and who exhibit a sense that one knows where they are coming from. The well-respected officers both give and get respect. Respect is a reflexive property, which recognizes others' rights and responsibility.

Weakness

A weak officer is one who cannot maintain a stable demeanor, who enforces no single set of rules, but instead is arbitrary in the application of the rules and one's relations on the shop floor. The weak officers are perceived to be unable to take care of themselves inside the walls and likely to cause trouble for everyone. They may lie to prisoners as well as staff. One officer says he always distrusts someone who will lie to an inmate because, "If he will lie to an inmate, he will lie to me."

Weak officers cannot be counted on in any emergency. Many officers report weak officers who "run the other way" when an alarm is activated. New officers, who have not had the opportunity to prove themselves, are often labeled as weak until some evidence of strength or respectability presents itself. Old-timers' reluctance to interact with newcomers is based on this prejudiced evaluation. In seeing that most newcomers do not have any "common sense," the old-timer is placing them in this category of weakness. The weak officers are also those who have not learned to say no and may often "front off" others by telling them yes, or worse, maybe. If there is little intention of fulfilling the request, saying yes is just a device to remove the immediate problem, not recognizing the damage their inability to say no causes.

Two specific officer types that are "weak" are found in the terms "snitch officer" and "PC" cop. In the parallel prisoner culture, a snitch is one who informs on others, often with personal gain as motivation. A "snitch officer" is one who cannot be trusted with information and is deemed unreliable by all. These officers are avoided in social and functional interactions. The relationship between the "snitch officer" and those to whom he is snitching also illustrates the power relations that exist in the hierarchy. The snitch officer passes information about other officers to the administration, generally in the hope of some personal gain. But the code of the prison, for officers and prisoners, negatively sanctions this informing. Just like the prisoner who hopes to gain something through informing, the officer's information may be used, but one gains little respect from this behavior.

The PC (Protective Custody) Officer is one who is perceived as unable to "take it." PC officers are seen as being afraid of the prisoners and the danger inherent in the job. These officers often receive posts that have little prisoner contact. Often the hospital is defined as a place for these workers who are unable to constructively deal with the tensions and the conflicts of the job. A longtime nurse in the hospital argues that many officers are placed in the hospital so "they are out of the way and so that we can babysit them." These workers, she argues, are unable to get along with prisoners or other staff and are shunted to the hospital to be under the informal eye of the civilian nursing staff.

In addition to the continuum between respected and weak officers, the interviews revealed the following additional types.

Rules and Regulations

This approach is characterized by a consistent application of the formal rules, a "no-nonsense" attitude, and a general lack of personal favoritism. While this category best fits the official image of the "professional correctional officer" presented in training, this officer does not place high within the power hierarchy of the prison. Entering the "power sweepstakes" of the prison requires strategy that is somewhat extracurricular and generally out of the perspective possessed by the rules and regs types. Prisoners report a positive attitude toward these officers because "You can always tell where they are coming from." Officers with two to three years experience can be placed in this type.

The Professional Correctional Officer is one of the subtypes of this category. With the advent of new job titles, an emphasis on increased training, and an occupational awareness fostered by the unions, this approach to the job is pursued by those with higher levels of education, and who desire to make a career within the Department of Corrections.

John Wayne

The John Wayne–Clint Eastwood type of officer was described as being a "tough guy," one who has to prove his authority. This type is out to gain as much power and status within the power hierarchy as possible. These workers are in their "badge heavy" period, and are seen as both humorous and dangerous by others with the "common sense" of the seasoned worker. These individuals approach every task with the goal of "making points," even at the expense of other officers. Generally these officers are not well respected by the prisoners as it may be at the prisoners' expense these workers make the points. Unfairness and discretionary decisions mark their strategies of getting through the day. "Asshole" is another term often applied to those who take this approach. In personal relations, male officers manifest a predatory attitude toward females and represent a macho attitude.

A subgroup of this type is known as the "gorillas," those whose emphasis on authority and violence is often needed, but not much admired, on the day-to-day job. Traditionally, the "goon" squad was a favorite position for these workers, but this has been phased out with the current heterogeneous squad. Women, it must be noted, often fit the image of the macho worker, even though the term must be linguistically stretched.

Wishy-Washy

This is a dangerous approach due to its unpredictable, discretionary, and inconsistent nature. These are the workers seen as being afraid of the inmates and the ones who have not learned to say no. Often newcomers will be labeled this type because they have not yet devised appropriate strategies for dealing with the conflicts and the contradictions of prison relationships. These workers last a short time, become "PC officers" or transfer to less threatening job assignments. Supervising officers, generally sergeants, "put the word out" on these workers and try to avoid having them work in their areas.

The Lazy/Laid-back Officer

This type of officer is perceived as being a little too close to the prisoners and may not be trusted. They may ignore simple security procedures and are judged to be incompetent and uncaring, as well as lazy. These officers are seen to be dangerous at worst, and worthless at best. "Dumptruck" or "airhead" are other terms used to describe those who cannot do the job and who do not pull their share on the shift. Another perspective defines these workers as laid-back, rather than lazy. Those who see these persons as laid-back interpret their lack of energy toward the job as a mellowness rather than laziness. Prisoners tend to like these officers because they can hustle their way across the tier without interference.

The All Right Officer

A type generally represented by old-timers, this approach is characterized by the ability to balance and reconcile the conflicts of the institution and the daily routine. These types of workers have developed the common sense to do the job but also recognize the limits of their authority over the prisoners and other workers. They have also come to accept their place in the hierarchy (not always without bitterness) and have developed a workable approach to the job. Prisoners generally have personal and positive relations with these workers and will seek their help in solving bureaucratic problems or special favors. Often these types of workers are judged as marginal in the eyes of the administration, particularly if they have several years of service with no promotion. Old-timers and youngsters can fall into this type. The old-timer in this category is perceived to have settled into a niche and as "just doing the job." A youngster may take on these characteristics through developing the "common sense" of the correctional worker in a short time and may be somewhat respected for this ability. The all right officers possess an intimate understanding of the mechanics of social control and have developed strategies of manipulating these processes. This manipulation serves their self-interests, rather than those of the administration. The all right officers are experts in reconciling the contradictions of the prison and reproduce social control on their own terms.

Dirty Cops

A dirty cop is the least respected member of this community, and like the "snitch" officer, is avoided and negatively perceived. Being dirty takes several forms, the most common are doing illegal "favors" for prisoners, carrying contraband (packing), and having intimate relationships with prisoners. "Packing" is evidently a rare but real occurrence and refers to bringing in contraband to prisoners. The nature of this contraband and the definition of "dirty" is flexible. By the official rules, giving any item not of state issue or already owned to a convict is illegal. Over time, workers develop their own situational definitions of contraband. For example, giving a convict a cigarette is clearly illegal, but many old-time officers report doing it on a regular basis. Sharing one's food is another common, but illegal, act.

The subjective definition of contraband is tied to the "common sense" of the worker, but also conveys distrust of other workers. The most serious form of packing involves drugs or weapons. The level of contraband in the institution as well as its source was difficult to determine. Other sources (Davidson, 1974) argue that a large amount of cash and drugs exists within the walls. Officials of the prison argue that most of the contraband is brought in by visitors and inmates who have access to the outside world. Still others admit that correctional workers (as well as other free people employed in the prison) are the source of a great amount of contraband.

Officers are often lured into packing by a small item which accelerates to blackmail and more serious contraband. Wright (1973, p. 92) describes one method through which officers are lured into carrying contraband. Dirty cops are a threat to personal and institutional safety. A dirty officer may also be one who develops an intimate relationship with prisoners. While generally this is most common to the female officers, there are some cases of homosexual males becoming involved with prisoners.

CONCLUSION

Common to all these types is the issue of predictability and reliability. In both daily routines and in emergency situations, all workers need to know the abilities, character, and reactions of those with whom they work. The dangerous potential of the job, the need to rely on others, and just the need to get through the day smoothly places a high value on predictability. The relationship to the central elements of prison culture is the second defining feature of these types. One's management of power relations shapes one's approach to the job and the perceptions held by others. One's penetration into the meaning systems attendant to prison culture, such as respect or weakness also influence behavior and perceptions. Each type and strategy of the correctional worker is directly related to the individual's alignment to the power structure and material interests, and abilities to get through the day. For example, the worker who is badge heavy, or a "macho cop," is primarily concerned with the pursuit of power to the exclusion of other issues. The "dirty cop" pursues individualized material interests (generally money), and the "all right" officer manages to balance these three focal concerns, just as he balances the conflicts and specific resolutions.

The third dimension of these types involves the development of common sense. The career stages and typologies discussed above are grounded in the contradictions and conflicts which shape the lived through experience of the correctional worker. At San Quentin, the common sense of the correctional worker is a result of reconciling the conflicts and the contradictions inherent in the prison world. Experience with the concrete problems of working in the prison allows some workers to develop such sense. Not all workers have this reconciliation, however, and thus are not perceived in a positive way. Common sense, for the prison worker, is the essence of a taken-for-granted worldview and represents successful penetration into the social structure and culture of the prison. Grounded in versions of behavior presented by the workers themselves, this typology provides a concrete understanding of activities and processes of social control.

6

The Reproduction of Social Control: The Worldview of the Prison Worker

The worldview of the prison worker is shaped by a system of relations, both with prisoners and among workers, and conflicts of interests specific to the prison. Each element can be described in terms of the definitions of the situation constructed through experience, interaction, and the distribution of power. In addition to one's negotiated relations, the distribution of power and authority determine one's place in this world. The worldview of the worker reflects a subjective penetration into the institutional order of the prison. The nature of social structure—in this case, social control—is thus revealed through the actions and meanings that underpin the workers' definitions of the prison. The reproduction of social control in the prison is dependent on the level of penetration into the culture of the prison and the internalization of these meanings by the individual worker. The extent to which each individual actor takes on these often contradictory meaning systems may also be dependent on microlevel variables such as age, gender, race, or preprison experiences. Much like the worldviews articulated by Irwin (1970) in *The Felon*, the worldview of the worker and his or her participation in the reproduction of social control is related significantly to extra-institutional factors. Similarly, one's experiences with other members of the prison community (workers, prisoners, and administrators), and the resulting relations determine the extent of penetration into these institutional forces of social control. One's penetration, therefore, shapes the manner in which each worker engages in this reproductive process. The concern here is with meaningful action. Understanding both symbolic and actual behavior traces individual perceptions of social terrains and subsequent participation in their reproduction.

Social control, like other reproductive processes, is negotiated and problematic. This negotiation occurs among like actors, situated within institutional contexts, often wielding unequal power within these contexts. The process of negotiation itself is a combination of power, interaction, and meaning. As illustrated in the discussion of the relations with prisoners, authority over the prisoners is never taken for granted. Instead, it is a subtle, reciprocal process which is negotiated through interaction and ideology. Unlike Sykes's (1958) conceptualization of the "corruption of authority," the reproductive perspective allows analysis of these relations through an intersection of interests rather than through the taint of "corruption." The members of the prison community, like other social beings, act according to socially constructed interests. Understanding the prison requires analysis of these interests and corresponding relations.

As a skilled performance of its constituent actors, the negotiation of social control is dependent on shared understandings about the world. Interaction and its corresponding relationships are grounded in these "practical theories" (Giddens, 1976) about the prison and its members. As Giddens argues, society, as a skilled performance of its members, is a human production, produced and reproduced anew through face-to-face interaction. These interactions are only possible because of mutual "stocks of knowledge," grounded in common meaningworlds. The activities of members in the prison community constitute the reproduction of social control.

POWER

Power and authority are central to the social order of the prison community. As a coercive institution, the prison operates in terms of authority over other human beings. As an intermediate in the formal stratification of the prison (Sykes, 1958), the correctional worker plays a pivotal role in the distribution of this power and authority. The worker is the point at which social control over the prisoners is delivered, but this relationship of power and authority is reciprocal. Prison workers, and their worldview, must be understood in the context of this power and authority and in terms of the ways in which they are both the subject and the object of social control. In delivering the power of the institution, correctional workers are also subjected to the effects of the very power exercised. The dominant role of power in shaping the perspective of the worker must by understood in terms of these constraints. While the prison worker has been traditionally characterized as an authoritarian personality, this image ignores the reflexive properties of power and social control.

In the prison, power directs relations among all members of the community. With prisoners, this power may take several shapes. Officially, the prisoners are subject to formal social control. Informally, oppression and brutality may shape these relations, but the evidence suggests that some unique forms of cooperation and reciprocity make up the majority of prisoner-staff relations. Among coworkers, these power relations are formally equal but are actually shaped by inequality. Knowledge of the system, personalized relationships, and other elements of the lived experience create unequal distribution of power among the line workers. Traditional power distribution, racist and sexist practices, and the personalized "dad and kid" relationships contribute to these inequalities.

While power and its distribution structure prison social order, interaction, and relations among the workers, administration and the prisoners provide the substance of this order. Interaction constitutes the lived experience of the prison worker and these encounters that construct definitions and meaningworlds. Approximately 75 percent of all correctional officer positions deal directly with prisoners. (Others, such as mail room or gun tower, deal indirectly with prisoners.) Developing a style that "gets along" with prisoners, maintains some semblance of discipline, and keeps the administration or superior officers satisfied with one's performance or at least, "off one's back" is the challenge of the correctional worker.

When starting the job, workers are puzzled as to how they will manage their prisoners. Over time these relations become the least problematic. Veteran workers define their relations with prisoners as a simple part of their jobs. These abilities to cope with prisoners become part of the taken-for-granted stocks of knowledge about the prison. Experience, interaction, and the development of a "common sense" makes these relations possible. The successful workers draw from a range of approaches and strategies to the job. These tactics are not static and all workers may modify their approaches given specific situations. These approaches signify the levels and degree of penetration into the institutional structure of social control. For example, the worker who keeps his distance through emphasizing the rules and regulations when working in a housing unit, may shift strategies when assigned to a small work crew. While consistency of style is highly valued, many workers possess a range of approaches to the job at hand. The concrete problems of the immediate job assignment determine one's approach to the situation and illustrate the negotiation of social control.

INTERACTION AND RESPECT

Interaction and "respect" are key features of the negotiation and reproduction prison social order. The successful correctional worker must learn how to work with prisoners and coworkers to accomplish the demands of the workday. The exact nature of one's experience with other prison community members determines the shape of these conceptions and contributes to the range of types and approaches to the job. Working with prisoners in work crews, overseeing visits or censoring mail, having day-to-day conversations to escape the boredom of the shift or obtain information creates practical meanings and relations on the shop floor of the prison. These encounters change the definitions of prisoners and in Sykes's words (1958, p. 55) cause the prisoners to be seen as a "man in prison rather than a criminal in prison and the relationships between the captor and the captive are subtly transformed in the process." Sykes characterizes this subtle transformation in terms of "claims of reciprocity" and the "corruption of authority," but other dimensions are necessary to explain the relationships between prisoners and workers. Interaction and meaning are the central features of this transformation and recognition of mutual interests is primary to the development of these relationships.

As the worker penetrates the institutional order of the prison, prisoners are no longer seen as abstract "inmates" but as individuals. The extent of this definition is related to the recognition of mutual interests. As workers and prisoners come to interact outside the bounds provided by the official definitions of these relations, they develop meanings specific to their own experience. As Blumer (1964) argues, the self is constituted through interaction with others. The self, for Blumer, is reflexive; interaction creates meanings, and meanings arise through interaction. Interpretation also shapes relations. Actions and meanings are central to the formation of the self and society. In the prison as well as in the outside world, social life is shaped by the activities and meanings of people meeting the conditions of their own lives. For the prison workers, the conditions of their lives are shaped by the nature of the job, the distribution of power and authority (both formal and informal), the traditions of the prison, and the relations with coworkers and prisoners that arise through interaction.

Adjusting to the new world of the prison, adapting to the demands of the job, and developing working relations with prisoners and coworkers occupies the time and energy of the worker. Learning to "fit in," as well as learning the physical layout and the policies and procedures of the job characterize the first phase of work. As one's career progresses, the worker may become "badge heavy" and may take to heart the authority of the position during this period of adjustment. Here, the individual worker best represents the pure essence of an agent of social control. The worker tests his abilities to use the tools of social control, trying on different strategies to determine their usefulness. The new worker may discover that this unilateral approach to relations with prisoners does not serve one's interest to get through the workday. The "badge

heavy" period does not last long, unless the worker comes to identify himself with institutional power struggles carried on by the
ruling clique. Some officers continue to be "badge heavy," primarily when they begin to align their self-interests with those of
the administration.

For the worker who becomes concerned with the concrete demands of the shop floor of the prison, and not with the politics of
the administration, a different set of interests develops. These
workers come to recognize the essential contribution interaction
and respect make to the social order of the prison. Over time, and
through daily experience, the worker absorbs this knowledge and
comes to recognize a set of interests not addressed in formal descriptions of the prison. The very nature of interaction on the job,
grounded in the prison value of respect, begins to erode this "badge
heaviness" through the evolution of new definitions about the job.

In addition to the problems of perspective, the recognition of
mutual interests with the prisoners presents other problems to the
correctional worker. This definition of the situation does not fit
with any other explicitly acknowledged perspective. The worker
may begin to doubt his abilities to do the duties of the correctional
worker. Many officers admit concern over their defining prisoners
as "friends." When this definition of the prisoner begins to shift
toward the more concrete many workers begin to look for other
jobs.

A very small minority of workers may come to take the interests
of prisoners more seriously. Characterized as the most dangerous
type of officer, these workers may agree to carry in contraband,
overlook serious rule violations, or otherwise take on the part of
the prisoner. Smuggling weapons or drugs is seen by all members
of the prison staff as extremely dangerous to the personal safety of
the workers and the "integrity" of the institution. Additionally,
such activity is also unsettling to the negotiated social order of the
prison. While all workers may struggle with the reconciliation of
conflicts and contradictions, the worker who becomes "dirty" becomes an outlaw of the staff. Such "outlaws," when discovered,
are fired from their jobs. Another form of recognizing these interests

takes the shape of "identifying" with the prisoners. This is an extreme form of "fraternizing" and is grounds for dismissal as well. Some workers may start to identify with the problems and the needs of prisoners and may step out of their assigned roles to address these needs and problems. This action may not be as extreme as the officer who smuggles contraband and weapons, but to the officials of the prison, such close relationships may be the first step toward becoming "dirty."

For the majority of workers, however, this conflict in perspectives lies within the acceptable range of perspectives. From the "badge heavy" officer to the "all right officer" these workers develop a perspective and a strategy that allows them to maintain relations with prisoners, do their job, and to fit in with the demands of social control. The distance between the world of the worker and the administration helps absorb some of these conflicts as well. The worldview of the correctional worker is thus shaped by the private reconciliation of these conflicts and contradictions. The development and identification of individual interests is also grounded in these relations. The competition for scarce resources, both material and social, shapes these perspectives and may contribute to the divisions along the line staff. The distribution of power, and the individual's perspective toward power and authority further structure the experience of the correctional worker.

COMMON SENSE AND DUTY

Two additional elements are necessary to the description of the worldview of the correctional worker. The most general description of the perspective of the correctional worker lies in the concept of duty. The military structure of the prison, the assigned positions, and the very nature of the work combine to produce a definition of the job that is expressed best in this idea. Tied to current conceptualizations of the prisoner, the law and order attitudes of the outside society and the trend toward "professionalizing" the role of the correctional institutions and the worker, this idea best accounts for the essence of the correctional worker.

The elements of the duty of the correctional officer are rendered in the everyday sense of the word. Duty has several dimensions when applied to the correctional worker. Duty implies a given set of responsibilities that are codified and systematic. Under the legal definition of the prisoner, such duty is required to ensure equal treatment of the prisoner. Second, duty implies a moral commitment to serve. In the sense that a duty is an obligation, both legal and moral, the position of the correctional worker is bound to the performance of such duty. This duty is toward society in general and toward the institution specifically. This state of being "bound" also explains the worker as both a subject and object of social control.

The chain of command which characterizes this bureaucracy of social control also reflects a sense of the word duty. Submission and obedience describes the location of the worker within this chain of command. While the worker is the point at which the social control function of the institution is delivered, the worker is also at the bottom of the prison's bureaucracy. While attending to submission and obedience of the prisoners, the correctional worker is also subject to obedience and submission to a set of policies set forth by the administration. The mandatory overtime, requirements of dress and demeanor and other elements of the militaristic social order illustrate these demands. The notion of duty also provides an understanding of the limits and constraints of the position. The moral or legal obligation to do a certain thing is present here, with the "certain thing" narrowly circumscribed by the policies of the administration. For the prison worker, due to the definition of the prisoner, duty is both moral and legal. The social control apparatus of the state insures its legality and the moral definition of the prisoner supplies the morality. The role of the prison worker, then, is narrowly constrained moral and legal duty. The constraints of duty also eliminate much of the free choice of the worker (even though in fact the job is characterized by extreme discretion over prisoners) and, in doing so, removed much of the responsibility from the worker. The idea of duty provides the worker distance and alleviates personal responsibility for his actions. The belief in duty allows the worker to rationalize any behavior done in the name of duty. These elements of distance and rationalization also legitimate the role and behavior of the correctional worker and place responsibility on the role rather than the individual worker.

Finally, the duty which describes the perspective and the role of the correctional worker is also a state of being. While occupied with the duties of the office and imbued with a legal and moral justification, the correctional worker represents a state of being that may exceed the walls of the prison. The development of this perspective on duty extends to the personal lives of the workers and continues to effect their meaningworld even when technically "off duty." The notion and the belief in duty, then, is the most general solution to the contradictions of meaning and social structure.

The "common sense" of the prison worker is the second element critical to this worldview. In addition to developing a sense of duty, the worker who successfully reconciles the conflicts of the job develops a common sense that is anything but common. Built up through experience and interaction, this common sense is only the result of a dense layer of theories about the prison and its members which have been tested and retested over time. This "sense" has been developed through interaction and cannot be handed down through training. New workers enter this world armed with a set of ideas about the prison and they are quickly disabused of them. This "common sense" is the discursive recognition of the worldview of the correctional worker. It is only complete after one has passed through these stages and is a source of conflict between workers who have mastered this world and those who do not. This common sense becomes the ideology of the correctional worker as it describes values, beliefs, and norms which inform the accomplishment of the job. As this "common sense" is based on a wide range of experiences and simply "doing time," it is unavailable to those who do not possess day-to-day experience. This conflict in perspectives divides experienced workers from new recruits and the line staff from the administration. Definitions of the nature of the job, of prisoners, or the "right" way to do the job are dependent on this "common" sense which is only common to a few. Of all the divisions among officers described above, it is this uncommon "common sense" that is the basis for most of the conflict between workers in the prison. The essence of this "common sense" appears to be a shared penetration into the reproductive mechanisms of social control.

As described above, the substance of this world is based on power, interaction, and a system of personalized relations. But the organization of these dimensions often creates conflicts and contradictions which must be solved in order to stay on the job. These conflicts may be institutionalized in forms such as racism, sexism, or through the power of an elite clique. The contradictions may appear as irreconcilable perspectives, which divide the workers and prohibit worker solidarity. The successful worker manages these conflicts and contradictions through the development of a particular worldview. The unsuccessful worker cannot make sense of the prison social world and fails to produce a perspective which solves the problems of the job. In short, the world of the correctional worker is tied directly to the meanings and relations which exist in the prison community. Through these meanings and relations, then, the reproduction of social control can be articulated. Operating within constraints of power and tradition, each worker must construct a worldview that rationalizes and "makes sense" of one's behavior. This worldview reflects degrees of penetration into the institutional forces in the contemporary prison and thus shapes the reproduction of social control.

Appendix 1: Discarded Images—A Literature Review

Understanding social control in the prison requires a specific examination of the prison worker. Research on the prison, however, has produced a rather uneven treatment of this member of the prison community. This discussion of the image of the worker focuses on the variety of ways the worker has been portrayed and moves toward the development of a new image of the worker. Like the prison itself, understanding of the correctional worker is confused by stereotypical popular images. These images have centered on the moral dimensions of the role and paid little attention to the dynamics of working in a prison. Investigation of the worker has been secondary to other prison issues, such as the social structure of the prison, its culture or the social organization of the prisoner community. The lack of information about the worker, combined with a secondary role in the literature leaves us with no coherent image of the correctional worker. A brief history of these images is necessary to set the stage for an understanding of the modern prison worker.

In the American eighteenth century, the prison emerged as a dominant means of punishment and social control. Other forms of punishment were neglected in favor of the emerging penitentiary (Rothman, 1971). The promises of the penitentiary and the corresponding images of the criminal were adopted throughout the new nation, as social control became centralized in the hands of the state (Tagaki, 1975). It was, as Rothman (1971) suggests, the age of the asylum.

Originally conceived as a place in which the offender would await judgment and punishment, the jail was not used as a place of long-term detention, or a punishment in itself. Like the European houses of detention (for examples, Ghent and Glouster), the first American jail, Walnut Street Jail, was modeled after the household. The jailor and his family were responsible for the care of those awaiting trial and the relationships with prisoners were grounded in this household model. An alternative model for these early institutions was the workhouse. The almshouse, the poorhouse, and other institutions of public welfare and social control were developed from these defining features.

The American prison drew some elements of its structure from these earlier institutional forms. The military model was the key feature in this new version of the prison. Discipline and order were the essence of social control. Rothman suggests that the military organization of the new prison affected the keepers as well as the convicts.

Several wardens came directly to their positions from an Army or Navy career—[the] legislators obviously eager to have them apply their former training to the setting. Guards wore uniforms, mustered at specific hours and kept watch like sentries. Regulations ordered them to behave in a "gentlemanly manner," like officers, without laughter, ribaldry or unnecessary conversation while on duty. As Sing-Sing's rules put it, in only a slight overstatement of the general sentiment: "They were to require from convicts the greatest deference and never suffer them to approach but in a respectful manner; they are not to allow them the least degree of familiarity, nor exercise any toward them, they should be extremely careful to command, as well as compel, their respect" (Rothman, 1971, pp. 106–7).

The strict rules for the workers produced elements of social control that were instituted reflexively. Not only was discipline to be applied to the prisoners, but to the workers as well. Rothman also describes the role of the worker in the age of the "turnkey" and in the early penitentiaries.

The ordinary guards would not have to be well-trained, for their contact with inmates would be slight and superficial; prisoners continuously confined to their cells would not have to be herded to meals or supervised in workshops or a common exercise yard. Security would be easily maintained . . . there would be little recourse to the whip . . . cruel punishment would be rare, because men in isolation would have little occasion to violate prison regulations. Finally, these arrangements would permit officials to treat prisoners as individuals. . . . The Pennsylvania penitentiary promised to be a secure, quiet, efficient, humane, well-ordered and ultimately reformatory institution (Rothman, 1971, p. 86).

PRISON RESEARCH

The next set of ideas about the prison comes during an era of intense investigation of the prison. This period, between the 1930s and the 1960s, produced diverse research on the prison and legitimized the field of study. The classic studies of the prisons, including Schragg (1944), Clemmer (1940), Haynor and Ash (1939), Wheeler (1961), Weinberg (1942), Sykes (1956, 1958), and the Social Science Research Council (Cloward, 1960) were conducted during this time.

The moral image of the worker was reinforced by the initial research. An early study suggests "The successful prison manager must be a real man; a moral force that is stronger than the inmates" (Stutsman, 1936, p. 63). Roucek (1935) described the job of prison guard in terms of its abnormality and isolation, the low morale of the work force and the loss of idealism of the young recruits. The authority structure of the prison, Roucek asserts, creates a "dangerous attitude" among the guards. This attitude is combined with "irksome and confining conditions" which are intensified "by a lack of a higher degree of intelligence and a lack of normal contacts" (Roucek, 1935, p. 149).

The best detail on the job itself comes from Clemmer's classic study of *The Prison Community* (1940). Using the concepts of primary group, culture, and the community to explain the prison social order, Clemmer also gives us a glimpse of the workround of the prison guard. He describes the duties of these jobs:

The duties vary from spending twelve hours alone in an isolated wall tower, to unlocking and locking a steel barred gate one thousand times a day. The guards are the wheel horses of the prison. They get the inmates up in the morning, march them to breakfast, dinner and supper, observe their work during the day, put them to bed at night and watch over them while they are sleeping. The duties are many and varied. While the actual physical work is small, the constant surveillance and caution they must exercise is nerve-wracking and tiring. As a group, the guards have little education and do not come from the "higher walks" of life (Clemmer, 1940, p. 62).

Clemmer also paints a picture of the prison guard as seen through the eyes of the prisoner:

The vernacular is always the same—the guard is a "screw" and so is the key with which he locks or unlocks the door . . . the term "screw" may come from the twisting motion used in unlocking or locking the door.

Some of the more derisive names are applied to the officials or guards, such as "Eagle Eye" to a watchful and alert deputy, "Red Muzzle" to a red faced deputy, "Butter and Eggs" to a prosperous looking and fleshy officer, "Nocky," "Chisel Chin," and "Bad Eye" to others (quoted in Clemmer, 1940, p. 92).

Relations between prisoners and workers are detailed by Clemmer. On one hand, the prison code of the convict dictates an adversarial relationship—one that is reported in later descriptions of the convict code (Irwin and Cressey, 1962; Sykes and Messinger, 1960). On the surface, the convict code, or "dogma" as Clemmer calls it, generates meanings that separate the worker and the prisoner. This dogma, he suggests, is a "prevalent attitude of hate and distrust of all penal officials" (Clemmer, 1940, p. 100). While most prisoners can only publicly report negative observations about the guards in general, some voice some private respect. For example, Clemmer reviews a story in which a misunderstanding occurred between a guard and a prisoner. The fact of the misunderstanding was regretted by the prisoner more than the actual punishment: "More than the punishment I hated the fact that the deputy who had used his influence on my behalf before thought I had broken my word" (Clemmer, 1940, p. 192). He closes this study of the prison community by suggesting: " . . . [P]risons work immeasurable harm on the men held in them as well as on the employees that care for them" (Clemmer, 1940, p. 316).

From this initial research, several principles form a basis for the study of the correctional worker. One, the moral definition of the worker, and the difficulty of working in the prison is given first voice in these early studies. Two, the drudgery of the job is described by Clemmer, suggesting that those doing this work are somehow ill-suited for other employment. This version of the worker is reflected in descriptions of the worker by the prisoners. This negative image of the worker persists today. At the same time, Clemmer's analysis provides a key to the study of the worker which also continues to shape inquiry into the worker.

THE SOCIAL SYSTEM OF THE PRISON

A third set of images of the prison was generated during research of the early 1960s. Much attention was focused on the idea of the social system of the prison. This work includes studies by Wheeler (1961), Cressey (1959, 1960), Cloward (1960b), Giallombardo (1966), Garabedian (1963), Goffman (1961), Irwin and Cressey (1962), McCleery (1961), Street (1965), and Sykes and Messinger (1960). Little direct attention is devoted to the prison worker, with the exception of Sykes and Cressey's work. Generally, the worker is discussed in the larger context of the prisoner culture. The emphasis on prisoner culture neglects a comprehensive understanding of the social order of the prison as a whole.

The image of the worker gained the most significant detail through the work of Sykes (1958) and Cressey (1959). Both efforts expand on the conflicts and contradictions foreshadowed by Clemmer. Cressey's work on the "contradictory objectives" of the prison (1959) suggests the cultural and institutional conflicts that shape relations on the shop floor of the prison. With the notion of "corruption of authority," Sykes underscores the importance of personal interaction among prisoners and workers and the contradictions set up by this interaction. These two concepts provide a framework for further analysis of the image of the prison worker.

The Corruption of Authority

In dedicating *Society of Captives* (Sykes, 1958) to "The man in prison—both the prisoner and his guard," Sykes recognizes the essential dependence between these two roles. Sykes sees that power and its distribution are fundamental to the prison order. The structural defects in this system of total power shape the position and the role of the prison worker. These defects produce a system of relations among the members of the prison community which illustrate the dynamics and the contradictions of the institution: "It is apparent then that the power of the custodians is defective, not simply in the sense that the ruled are rebellious, but also in the sense that the rulers are reluctant" (Sykes, 1958, p. 58).

The origins of these defects and the implications of this reluctance are traced throughout the study. Sykes sees that the prison, as the most "modern rational form of mobilizing efforts to exercise social control and the use of physical violence" makes the prison official a bureaucrat, "but he is a bureaucrat with a gun" (Sykes, 1958, p. xv).

Several dimensions combine to create these structural defects in the theoretical "total power" of the administration. First, for policy and political reasons, the administration cannot exercise its right to physical violence in every case. Second, the few rewards and resources available to the prisoners are already distributed as a matter of course, so little incentive exists to motivate conforming behavior. Third, prisoners do not generally recognize the authority of the prison to dictate their behavior. Finally, the very nature of the work forces worker and prisoner to interact in a wide range of situations and leads to the development of patterns of social relations. For example, the need for prisoner labor in the maintenance of the prison and this social interaction shape this corruption of authority.

It is these patterns of release and reconfinement which set the stage for a wide range of interaction between inmate and inmate, and guard and inmate; and in this interaction we can begin to see the realities of the prison social system emerge (Sykes, 1958, p. 6).

The daily contact that is structured in the roles of worker and prisoner contributes to a definition of the situation that may operate independently of the formal roles. This interaction, this crossing of roles, is the origin of the corruption of authority.

The expected role of the guard, then, is a complicated compound of policeman, of cadi, and foreman, counsellor and boss all rolled into one. But as the guard goes about his duties, piling day on top of another (and the guard too, in a certain sense, is serving time in confinement), we find that the system of power is defective not only because the means for motivating the inmates to conform is largely lacking but also because the guard is frequently reluctant to enforce the full range of institutional regulations. The guard frequently fails to report infractions of the rules that have occurred right before his eyes. The guard often transmits forbidden information to the inmates, such as plans for searching particular cells in a surprise raid for contraband. The guard often neglects elementary security requirements and on numerous occasions he will be found joining his prisoners in outspoken criticisms of the warden and his assistants. In short, the guard frequently shows evidence of having been "corrupted" by the captive criminals over whom he stands in theoretical dominance (Sykes, 1958, p. 54).

The sources of this corruption are tied to the very structure of the job itself. The "close and intimate association with the prisoners" creates relationships between prisoners and workers that transcend the bounds of the role. The pressures from American culture to "be a good Joe, a nice guy" and the intermediate, often powerless position of the worker combine with a "basic ambivalence toward the prisoner" to cause the inmate to be seen as a "man in prison rather than a criminal in prison and the relationships between the captor and the captive are subtly transformed in the process" (Sykes, 1958, pp. 54–56). Thus Sykes constructs a new image of the prison worker. This image sees the worker as subjected to the demands of the prison bureaucracy as well as the more subtle demands of social relationships.

Contradictory Objectives: The Case of the Prison

Cressey addresses the basic conflicts in his article, "Contradictory Objectives in Complex Organizations: The Case of the Prison" (1959). The role of the worker, he argues, embodies the problem of the prison: "This role is dependent on the organizational goals and often reflects the contradictory directives of the modern correctional institutions" (Cressey, 1959, p. 477). In the administration's view, prisoners were viewed as "dangerous, scheming, conniving men in need of close surveilance" (Cressey, 1959, p. 481). Workers were prohibited from "unnecessary conversations with inmates" and were warned against its consequences. But, once out of the earshot of the administration, many of the older guards ignored this prohibition. As one experienced worker is quoted remarking to a new worker: "I talk to them all the time. How in the hell are you going to get anything done if you do not talk to them? To hell with them [the administration], just keep talking to them" (Cressey, 1959, p. 485).

These comments point to the contradictory objectives suggested by Cressey. On one hand, the guard is to guard—to enforce the rules and treat prisoners equally and consistently. On the other hand, the guard was expected, and required, to minimize the number of disgruntled inmates and "to use discretion and common sense in enforcing the rules" (Cressey, 1959, p. 483). This gap between the expectations of the administration and the reality of getting through the workday with prisoners creates a final contradiction for the worker. Cressey sees that:

It became impossible for the guards to find a principle for committing their energy to following rules, to using common sense and discretion, or to an acceptable combination of the two (Cressey, 1959, p. 489).

This split is also recognized by the administration. Cressey quotes one top administrator as saying, "I have more trouble from the guards around here than I do from the inmates" (Cressey, 1959, p. 487).

In reflecting on this era of research, Irwin (1980) suggests two ways in which prisoners and workers structure their relations: "personal agreement and corrupt favoritism." Following Sykes, Irwin sees that the use of direct physical force is limited. The popular image of brutal force, he suggests, is somewhat exaggerated, because, simply, these strategies of social control are unsuccessful in maintaining order over time. However, the lack of any consistent use of beatings and other physical assaults does not suggest that such actions were absent from the prison, but rather an individualized response. "When guards did employ corporeal punishment, more often they were expressing their own sadism or exaggerating the attitude toward prisoners—[that] the prisoners were subhuman" (Irwin, 1980, p. 22).

Both personal agreement and corrupt favoritism fit the idea of reciprocity as described by Sykes (1958). Each implies a specific relationship between worker and prisoner that exceeds the formal roles dictated by the formal structure of the institution and the "convict code." Personal agreements imply an "explicit or tacit agreement with prisoners in which the latter would refrain from rule-breaking in return for some special dispensation" (Irwin, 1980, p. 22). Corrupt favoritism was a situation in which "guards granted special privileges in return for their support in maintaining order" (Irwin, 1980, p. 23).

While the prison worker rarely occupied center stage in the continuing analysis of the prison, a careful review of these studies allows a partial reconstruction of the role. From the early images supplied by Clemmer (1940) and Roucek (1935), Sykes (1958), and Cressey (1959) move toward an institutional explanation of this role. Here is an image of a role caught up in the structural forces of the prison. The nature of worker-prisoner interaction and the dynamics of social control provide a context for future work.

THE CONTEMPORARY IMAGE:
REHABILITATION AND CORRECTIONS

The reintroduction of the rehabilitative ideal and the indeterminate sentence (Irwin, 1980; Fogel, 1979) altered the thrust of social control in the prison. Beginning in the 1950s, treatment became the rule of the day. The idea of rehabilitation is not a new idea. The Auburn and Pennsylvania penitentiary systems were originally founded on the premise of rehabilitation. The role of the worker in this process was not clear. During the Progressive Era of penal reform, the role of the worker was highlighted. Fogel (1979, p. 30) quotes from a prominent speaker at a national prison reform conference " . . . all future reforms are tied to the transformation of the guard into a trained professional. All programs are dependent on the guard. If he were transformed, prison reform should follow as surely as the oak wrapped around the acorn."

In the 1940s and 1950s, the revival of the rehabilitative ideal introduced the concept of pathology to definitions of the prisoner. This image supported a clinical model of "corrections" and implied the notions of sickness and treatment. This treatment was to be delivered by a new wave of workers, most importantly the "correctional officer" and a staff of counselors and psychologists. The definition of individual pathology provides the justification for the medical model of corrections that emerged after the era of the Big House. In defining the convicted criminal as "in need of help," a range of treatment strategies was developed within the context of the new correctional institutions. The implications of treatment, and the attending definitions of the prisoner provided an unlimited amount of power to the prison and its officials. This power and control over the prisoner took place within the "total institution" and was rarely subjected to public or judicial review. The lack of power of the prisoners further isolated the structure and function of the prison from the larger society.

California was one of the first systems to implement seriously the tenets of the rehabilitative ideal. In a history of Soledad Prison, Yee (1973) provides a description of this shift. Under Governor

Earl Warren (1942–53) a change in the organization of California prisons began. After an investigation of the state's prisons, Warren called a special session of the state's legislature to remedy the problems. "He knew that conditions were bad but the detailed accounts of depravity and sadism and squalor which were commonplace in the state's penal institutions convinced him that the system had to be discarded and completely reorganized" (Yee, 1973, p. 2).

The key change in this new policy revolved around the "new" concept of rehabilitation and the indeterminate sentence system. This allowed the prison authorities to make a judgment on the "rehabilitation" of the prisoner through setting release dates. The mechanisms for producing "rehabilitation" included correctional counselors, classification systems, and a variety of vocational and educational programming. As part of this trend, a change of symbolism reflected the changing conceptions of prisons and their prisoners. As Yee notes:

Along with the new reforms came a new terminology. Henceforth, guards would be called "correctional officers." The term lent dignity. Prisons would be called "correctional training facilities." Convicts or prisoners would be called "inmates" and "residents," men who were "housed" or "in custody" instead of using "imprisoned" or "incarcerated." The rehabilitation process of education, vocational training and counseling would be called "treatment." "Correctional officers" were in charge of "custody." "Counselors" were concerned with "treatment." If the inmates broke rules and had to be punished with closer confinement, they would no longer be placed in dungeons, but in "Adjustment Centers," the Orwellian term for maximum security cell blocks which were built to house the most recalcitrant inmates (Yee, 1973, p. 4).

As the official image of the prisoner was altered through institutional definitions, a corresponding change took place with the definition of the prison worker. The new "correctional officer" held the hope of the entire new system of prison reform. Yee compares these expectations.

To change the attitude of prisoners, McGee first had to change the attitudes of his guards. The changes had to go far beyond a simple change of title. As one of McGee's protege's explained it, "The old-time guard, gun guard or turnkey could force behavior but he could not change attitudes. In fact, he was apt to make situations worse." While the correctional officer was still responsible for the custody of the prisoners under his charge, he was now supposed to give the convict as much "freedom" as possible to offset the debilitating boredom of cell life. The new "correctional officer" was to do this "by his own impact and fair treatment practices through leadership rather than resorting to severe punishments." The new correctional officers were of course, the same old guards (Yee, 1973, p. 5).

THE CURRENT IMAGE

In the thirty years since this change of title, the "correctional officer" has received renewed attention. A separate body of research concentrates on the role of the worker and examines this role in the context of the changing context of the American prison. Philliber (1987, p. 9) reviews this literature and notes a resurgence of the negative image of the worker.

As research on guards has gained momentum, a new set of descriptors that is no less pejorative has emerged. A review of the current research yields the distinct impression that COs are alienated, cynical, burned out, stressed but unable to admit it, suffering from role conflict of every kind and frustrated beyond imagining.

The work that creates contemporary images of the correctional worker can be summarized in terms of several themes. The negative image of the work is reinforced through liberal critiques of the role, the emphasis on the authoritarian personality, and research findings on job stress and job dissatisfaction, role conflict. The changing demographics of the work force is described in work on race and gender relations. Unionization efforts point to efforts to gain some control over the job.

British Studies

Studies of the correctional worker in Britain provide a comprehensive overview of these themes. Thomas (1972) traces the evolution of the English prison officer in an historical survey of the role. The seeds of structural and role conflict are based on the shift in organizational definitions and goals of the English prison system. As these goals began to shift from security and control to treatment and rehabilitation, the worker was caught up in the conflicts brought about by these changes. An earlier study of Pentonville (Morris and Morris, 1963) makes a similar point. Their investigation of a traditional, maximum security prison suggests that the conflict of roles for staff is related to competition over scarce resources. The prison staff, primarily the "screws," feel the pressure of this competition. Within this framework, Morris and Morris provide detail, much like Clemmer (1940) on the nature of the work.

Morris and Morris also describe the "common culture" held by prisoners and workers. Suggesting that workers themselves are subjected to the effects of "prisonization" (cf., Clemmer, 1940), the demands of the job also affect the personal lives of the workers.

Smith-Merrow (1962) provides one of the few lengthy first-person descriptions of the job. As a prison worker for 32 years, Smith-Merrow argues that the position is indeed a "thankless one" (p. 3) and takes exception to the rehabilitative philosophy and suggests that "compassion and kid-glove treatment" are "utterly out of place when it comes to handling thugs of the worst type" (Smith-Merrow, 1962, p. 14).

The themes suggested above are spread throughout a diverse literature of the American prison. Most familiar are the "liberal" critiques of the role. Wright (1973) and Mitford (1971) are good examples of this critical treatment of the worker.

Liberal Critiques

Mitford (1971) offers the least rigorous of the two critiques. Relying on anecdotal evidence, her chapter on "The Keeper and the Kept" suggests that guards are somewhat defective in that they come to work in the prison in the first place. She tells the story of a "friend with a degree in social welfare" who applied for the advertised position of "correctional officer" because he thought it "sounded like, really constructive, humanitarian work" (Mitford, 1971, p. 6). The friend was horrified to discover that the position was really that of a prison guard. Mitford suggests that this horror was justified by what she terms the "guard mentality." She makes much of the "guard's mentality" without ever defining the meanings of the term. The intent, however, is clear. Mitford quotes Eugene Debs as evidence of her position of the worker.

The guard and the inmate cease to be human beings when they meet in prison. The one becomes a domineering petty official and the other a cowering convict. The roles enforce this relation and absolutely forbid any intimacy of the human touch in it between them. The guard looks down on the convict he has now at his mercy, who has ceased to be a man and is known only by his number, while, little as the guard may suspect it, the prisoner looks down upon him as being even lower than an inmate (Eugene Debs, from *Walls and Bars* quoted in Mitford, 1971, p. 8).

The majority of guards, she suggests, are white, middle-class, and rural with few occupational skills.

Thus many become guards because they have no other choice of livelihood. Their pay is low, the civil service standards are minimal [and] they are generally considered to be at the bottom of the law-enforcement barrel. A reading of recent congressional hearings on prison conditions reveals, not unexpectedly, that beyond those men and women who become guards because they have no alternative, this occupation appeals to those who like to wield power over the powerless and to persons of sadistic bent (Mitford, 1971, p. 10).

While grounded in a more empirical study, the image of the worker provided by Wright (1973) also supports this tradition. Wright stresses the view of the prison officials and draws primarily on the perspective of those in power within the formal structure of the prison. He describes the administration's conception of the ideal prison guard, a firm but fair worker who is respected by the prisoners. This "firm but fair" image, Wright suggests, is echoed in the rules for new employees. The administration is convinced that following the rules provides a comprehensive framework for all action on the job (Wright, 1973). He discusses the differences between treatment and custody staff.

First of all, guards are under pressure in the prison system very different from those of non-custodial employees. They are directly responsible for the control of prisoners, and they bear the brunt of criticism when the control breaks down. Second, it would seem likely that the sort of person who chooses to become a prison guard differs from one who becomes a counselor, a chaplain or a teacher, and that this is reflected in attitudes toward the role of the prison. It would be expected that guards would tend to be more authoritarian than non-custodial employees, that they would have a stronger internal need to dominate and control other people, and that in many cases they become guards in the first place at least in part to fulfill those needs (Wright, 1973, p. 74).

Wright chooses to continue the tradition of locating the motive for working in the prison within the personalities of the workers alone. This image of a "different sort of person" continues to characterize the image of the correctional worker, just as the individual deviance of the criminal is stressed.

THE AUTHORITARIAN PERSONALITY

This emphasis on personality locates the cause of "authoritarianism" in the prison within the individuals. While personality tests and prediction factors for the prisoner are a traditional part of the rehabilitative ideal (Irwin, 1980), only recently has this idea been applied to the workers themselves. Goldstein (1975) explores these tests and concludes that standardization of recruitment and hiring practices by correctional institutions is one solution to this concern. However, her research suggests that standard personality and vocational interest tests do not measure accurately the characteristics of a competent correctional worker. Goldstein (1975, p. 5) quotes a 1968 study which attempted to use the Minnesota Multiphasic Personality Inventory and the Strong Vocational Interests Test to differentiate between "good" officers and "bad" officers. This study concludes that these standard measures are not significantly correlated with job performance. Additionally, a nationwide study cited in Goldstein (1975, p. 7) found little correlation between high scores on entry exams and superior job performance. In sum, the evidence using standard personality measures does not support the idea that prison workers, as a class, possess any personality traits which lead to authoritarianism.

In an experimental attempt to answer this question, Haney, Banks, and Zimbardo (1973) conducted an experiment around these issues. This experiment, popularly known as the Zimbardo experiment, attempted to test for evidence of the "guard mentality, a unique syndrome of traits that they bring to the situation which engenders the inhumane treatment of prisoners" (Haney et al., 1973, p. 69). This experiment took two matched groups of volunteers and randomly assigned each male to the "guard" group or the "prisoner" group. The nature and the content of their interaction was then analyzed and the authors concluded that: " . . . we witnessed a sample of normal, healthy American college students fractionate into a group of prison guards who derived pleasure from insulting, threatening, humiliating and dehumanizing their peers . . . " (Haney et al., 1973, p. 84). They also found that, "Most dramatic and distressing to us was the ease with which sadistic behavior could be elicited in individuals who were not sadistic types" (Haney et al., 1973, p. 84). This study found that the role of the guard carried with it "social status within the prison, a group identity . . . and above all the freedom to exercise an unprecedented degree of control over the lives of other human beings [and that] the use of power was self-aggrandizing and self-perpetuating" (Haney et al., 1973, p. 88). This experiment, the authors suggest, also gave rise to a normative culture among the "guard" group which defined strength and weakness according to power.

Not to be tough and arrogant was seen as a sign of weakness by the guards, and even those good guards who did not get drawn into the power syndrome as others did, respected this implicit norm of never contradicting or even interfering with the actions of a more hostile guard on their shift (Haney et al., 1973, p. 90).

This study shifts its explanation away from the pathological qualities of the workers' personalities to the "pathological situation" of the prison itself. The differences in behavior between the "guard" and the "prisoner" groups is explained through ". . . the result of an intrinsically pathological situation that could distort and re-channel the behavior of essentially normal human beings." That is, it is not the worker that is abnormal, but the situation itself: "The abnormality here resided in the pathological nature of the situation and not in those who pass through it" (Haney et al., 1973, pp. 84–85).

Advocates for the worker maintain that this abnormality of working conditions contributes to occupational stress (Brodsky, 1977), the need for higher standards and "professionalization" of the role and may also provide some impetus to the trend toward unionization among correctional employees (Wynne, 1978; Jacobs and Crotty, 1978). Highlighting the social and institutional effects and the "nature of the situation" has given rise to a more sociological, rather than characterological examination of the role.

THE SOCIAL CONTEXT

More recently, the worker has been investigated within the social context of the prison. These current investigations suggest several dimensions of the role of the worker and his or her relation to the prison community. Stress, job dissatisfaction, and role conflict continue investigation of the negative aspects of the work. Unionization efforts are described as one response to these issues. Work on race and gender relations and officer subcultures round out the examination of the changing social context.

Stress

"Occupational stress" has been used to explain a wide range of problems associated with employment in the prison. Thacker (1979) characterizes job-related stress in terms of job burn out. For the correctional worker, this is manifested in a loss of emotional concern and results in the treatment of prisoners in "detached and dehumanized ways" (Thacker, 1979, p. 34). He argues that stress disability contributes to low morale, absenteeism, high job turnover, substance abuse (drug and alcohol), mental illness, marital failure, and suicide.

One response to this occupational stress is what Thacker calls "going by the book" and the rationale that one is "only doing my job." He suggests that the existence of an "institutional macho code" prohibits the worker from expressing any emotions over the job and channels workers' emotions into psychosomatic illnesses. Cheek and Miller (1982) report similar findings. In New York State, for example, correctional officers' time off for disabilities is 300 percent higher than the average time off taken by other state employees. Cheek and Miller suggest that this high level of stress is somehow related to the low self-esteem of the worker and is related to a lack of clear job descriptions, inadequate equipment, and an overall lack of training.

Brodsky (1977) compares the incidents of stress between correctional workers and schoolteachers and found that their common position of "institutional buffer" generates similar demands and tensions which becomes translated through stress disabilities. This stress he argues, in line with Cressey's analysis of contradictory objectives, is caused by confused organizational goals: "Prison guards, too, are custodial officers in an institution about which society has not made up its mind" (Brodsky, 1977, p. 134). For the correctional workers, one of the key elements leading to a stress-related disability was the sudden recognition of the conflicts and contradictions in the system itself. This was especially difficult for the correctional workers in that most of the surveyed workers had what Brodsky calls "pro-system personalities" and had histories of "hyperadaptive behaviors." Most of the workers seen by Brodsky possessed what he calls a "conventional syndrome" of personality traits. Precipitating their crisis response was a developing awareness of the conflicts inherent in their jobs. A lack of cohesiveness among coworkers and overt conflicts with the administration were major causes of stress-related episodes: For Brodsky, a stress reaction is a "traumatic neurosis" which disables the worker when confronted with a work environment that no longer "makes sense" to the worker (Brodsky, 1977, p. 138).

This aspect of literature makes the transition from an individualized explanation of the worker's role to a more contextual description. Cullen et al. (1985) list contextual elements that contribute to work stress which include role conflict, perceptions of danger, working in a maximum security institution, female gender, level of experience, and lack of support from supervisors, peers, and family.

Role Conflict and Job Dissatisfaction

The structural conflicts of the job find expression in studies of role conflict and job dissatisfaction. For example, Pogrebin (1978) suggests this role is ambiguous because of a discrepancy between the workers' perception of the role and the way one is required to carry it out. The lack of clear job definitions and objective standards of job performance is another source of this role conflict (Thomas, 1972). Overall, however, the concept of role stress centers on the contradictory objectives of treatment and custody. Hepburn and Albonetti (1980) found that this conflict is highest in minimum security facilities, where the relative freedom and lower classification of the prisoners lead to an ambiguous definition of the situation. Role stress itself is often related to both years in service and to educational attainment (Poole and Regoli, 1980). They also found that custody orientation was related positively to number of years in service and negatively to increased education.

Developing relations with prisoners are related to the conflict in the role. Ross (1981) describes "problem-solving conspiracies" with prisoners that were seen to be a compromise of the traditional custody role. This compromise created a gap between initial expectation and the need to get through the work day. Johnson (1981) asserts that guards are often in a no-win situation as a result of this role conflict. As the job creates a continuum between mundane routine and potential violence, each worker is unsure of one's position in the prison social order. This analysis follows Cressey's image of the "contradictory objectives" of the prison. Other forms of conflict have been documented elsewhere. Cheatwood (1974) sees that the correctional worker is caught between the administration and the inmates. Zald (1962) sees that the conflict between treatment and custody is played out in role conflict for the prison staff.

Job dissatisfaction appears to be located in the low status of the position, both within the prison and in the larger society (Stotland, 1976; Jacobs and Zimmer, 1980). On the other hand, Toch and Klofas (1982) found little evidence of role conflict, but found that alienation was a key issue among the workers. Poole and Regoli (1981) found that measures of alienation were related to negative attitudes toward other members of the prison community, including coworkers, administrators, and inmates.

Unionization Efforts

These issues have led to a growing movement toward unionization among correctional workers. This move can be seen as a formal step to decrease the feelings of powerlessness that accompany the role. Jacobs and Crotty (1978) argue that the traditional reluctance of this occupational group to organize is overcome by a rising dissatisfaction with the manner in which the prison is administered. While questioning the compatibility of collective bargaining with the paramilitary structure of the prison, Jacobs and Crotty see that such issues as job safety and seniority contribute to this unionization movement. Potter (1979) suggests that unionization is a result of workers becoming more "class conscious," more militant, and may in fact be a reaction against what they see as contempt by the public and prisoners. Staudohar (1976) suggests five reasons that correctional employees seek collective bargaining agreements: employee safety; recruitment practices, including seniority; legal issues; competition from several unions; and low pay.

While the movement toward unionization can be tied to the general trend of public employee unionization, the increase in prisoner rights has also contributed to this development (Wynne, 1978; Montilla, 1978; and Jacobs and Crotty, 1978). As the civil and legal rights of the prisoners were restored by the courts in the 1970s (Fogel, 1979) the workers began to see that their authority was in danger of eroding. Collective bargaining agreements were viewed as one method of protecting workers' rights. Additionally, and perhaps more importantly, union activity was seen as a reaction to discretionary administrative decisions. Unions generally deal with salary and fringe benefits, sick leave abuse, seniority, promotions and job assignments, and employee grievance procedures. Significantly, prisoner-related issues are secondary to the more general labor-management conflicts. For example, in 1973, Massachusetts workers were "outraged over new inmate disciplinary procedures which included procedures by which inmates could call officers as witnesses, reduced the number of formal disciplinary actions against inmates and chose to deal with infractions through more informal methods" (Montilla, 1978, p. 348). Other "job actions" were involved with demands for "hazardous duty pay" for positions involving contact with prisoners, implementation of programs for prisoners with increasing job positions to insure adequate coverage, and other safety-related issues. By and large, most union issues center on employee-management issues, such as length of the work week, tuition and educational support, uniform allowance, and recruitment standards. Politically, correctional employee unions have also served a lobbying function, particularly with state legislatures. For example, Pennsylvania correctional unions have lobbied for increased policy input, longer prison terms, and more stringent parole guidelines (Montilla, 1978, p. 360). It is possible, however, to separate such political demands from economic concerns that would ensure job security and increased number of positions for union members.

Unions can also be understood in terms of the distribution of power and authority within the institution. Jacobs and Crotty (1978) suggest that unionization has shifted power away from the administration, and in some ways, has redefined the adversarial relations in the prison. Previously, workers may have defined the prisoners as their primary adversaries. Under the new shape of labor relations, the administration is cast as the adversary over the significant power issues. This shift in adversarial relations also suggests that workers and prisoners may begin to recognize their common interests (Jacobs and Crotty, 1978). Issues of safety in the prison, more comprehensive coverage, increased staff for programs and overcrowding would benefit prisoners as well as workers.

Race and Sex in the Pen

While unions may represent the general interests of the workers in terms of labor relations, there is some evidence that the union structure reproduces the traditional barriers against women (Zimmer, 1986) and minorities. For example, many unions have filed suits against correction department affirmative action programs on the grounds of "reverse discrimination" (Wynne, 1978, p. 2) and have expressed opposition over the hiring of women workers in "sensitive" jobs. Furthermore, union leaders are most often white males.

Jacobs (1979) illustrates the issues surrounding opposition to women workers in discussing a Supreme Court decision (*Dothard* v. *Rawlinson*). In this case, the U.S. Supreme Court upheld Alabama's hiring policy which excluded women on the basis of height and weight standards. Other court cases have also addressed the issue of strength, sexual abuse by prisoners, prisoner constitutional rights to privacy, and other legal concerns. Overall, staff members report to be concerned with female workers' abilities to subdue violent prisoners, conform with standards of prison discipline, and the gender perspective of women in general (Kissel and Siedel, 1980; Jacobs, 1979). In a cross-cultural examination of women workers, which centers on Finland, Antilla (1975) counters arguments that suggest women may be unable to work in male institutions due to their "inability to maintain order in the criminal justice system, as related to their sexual insecurity and lack of understanding of male criminality" (p. 72). This study also found that women workers generally adapt to the accepted beliefs and traditions and conform to the perspective of their male colleagues. Crouch and Alpert (1980) see that women tend to be less negative about inmates over time, whereas men tend to become more negative. Jurik's work (1985a, b) looks at attitudes of male and female workers. She found that attitudes about inmates were generally not tied to gender. She does suggest that the visibility of women workers contributes to a sensitivity over their performance. Cullen et al. (1985) found that women seem to have higher levels of stress.

Zimmer (1986) provides significant information on the experience of female workers in male institutions. She describes three strategies that women develop to meet the personal and organizational challenges confronted by women guarding men. The institutional role is somewhat similar to a rules and regulation approach. The modified role takes into account one's gender and adjusts to these perceived differences. The inventive role combines aspects of custody and counseling.

Race

In addition to gender, race has become a source of conflict for prison workers (Jacobs and Kraft, 1978; Carroll, 1977). Racial prejudice of the workers toward the prisoners is an often-cited reason for prison brutality (Attica Commission Report, 1972; Irwin, 1980). However, the interaction between race and the roles of worker and prisoner remain unclear. On one hand, some research suggests that minority staff members will alleviate some of the racial hostility between prisoners and staff. On the other hand, others suggest that the status of correctional workers will supersede any racial solidarity. Jacobs and Kraft express this question concisely:

The assumption is that because minority prison guards have the same economic and cultural background as the minority prisoners, they will treat them more humanely and relate to them more effectively. It is also assumed that the minority prisoners will view the authority of the minority guards as more legitimate.

A contrary hypothesis, drawn from the sociology of occupations, suggests that the role demands on the prison guard are both so encompassing and restrictive that all guards, regardless of social background and prior beliefs, will inevitably develop hostile attitudes toward prisoners (Jacobs and Kraft, 1978, p. 306).

In surveying 231 correctional workers in Illinois, Jacobs and Kraft (1978) found that there was no significant difference between black and white workers in terms of behavior or attitudes toward minority prisoners. Crouch and Alpert (1980) report similar findings. Cullen et al. (1985) report, however, that blacks are more likely to be dissatisfied with their work.

The image of the correctional worker as white, rural, and male (Mitford, 1971; Jacobs and Retsky, 1975), is inaccurate in light of the affirmative action practices of the last decade. Examination of the effects of affirmative action on both the power structure of the prison and the subculture of the worker would contribute more accurately to the image of the correctional worker (Owen, 1985). Beard (1975; National Bar Association, 1978) found that minorities are seriously underrepresented in management and supervisory positions throughout corrections. Jones (1978) suggests that the number of black recruits has increased dramatically since the early 1970s (p. 9). Minority employee associations have developed in partial response to this underrepresentation (Jones, 1978).

RECENT STUDIES

In response to the lack of comprehensive information on the correctional worker's role, recent studies have attempted to describe the position in detail. In contrast to the indirect information provided in past research on the prison, this work concentrates on the worker as the primary topic of investigation.

In attempting to address the inadequate image of the worker, Lombardo (1981a) describes the working world of the correctional worker. He addresses the "focal concerns" of the worker and constructs the "internal motivations" that lead to one's occupation as a correctional worker. For example, most workers report that while the nature of the work is not particularly attractive, compared to other employment options and considering the pay and job stability of the work, employment at the prison may in fact be a good opportunity. The workers also report feeling that it is hard for "outsiders" to understand the job and their feelings about it.

Most workers enter this job with little idea as to its exact nature. Lombardo suggests that most workers find their initial impressions contradicted upon employment, especially those images and definitions of prisoners (Lombardo 1981a, p. 27). Prisoners are often the primary source of information for the new workers. Lombardo argues that relations with prisoners are central to successful job performance. The new workers must learn how to deal with their formal authority in a way that is conducive to the operation of the prison culture. For some workers this may mean developing a human service approach, solving prisoner problems or cutting through red tape, for example. Other approaches to the job include order maintenance, security, rule enforcement, and supervisory roles.

Relations among workers are also examined. Unlike relations among police officers, there was little evidence of an apprentice-like relationship between older and younger workers. The competition for "good jobs" divided the workers, although the introduction of a bidding system decreased this source of conflict. The hardest part of the job, according to Lombardo's sample, is "putting up with people who mess with you" (p. 62).

The correctional workers in Lombardo's study had a remarkably low turnover. This is in direct contrast to other prisons that have a high turnover ranging from 20 to 80 percent (Jacobs and Grear, 1977). Lombardo concludes that the real product of the job is a smoothly functioning work area which may in fact be the result of informal accommodations between workers and prisoners. Like Sykes, Lombardo suggests that it is reciprocity between worker and prisoner that accounts for the social order of the prison.

In her book, *Women Guarding Men*, Zimmer (1986) opens a new area of inquiry into the heterogeneity of the prison work force. This study of female officers in male prisons echoes previous findings of gender-based conflicts (Owen, 1985; Jurik, 1985a) and details the types of strategies developed by women workers. Zimmer suggests that female officers may in fact be more innovative as they confront the problems of working in the pen.

CONCLUSION

The literature of the prison has only recently examined the role of the correctional worker. Building on a tradition begun in *The Prison Community* (Clemmer, 1940), contemporary descriptions of the prison have cast the worker in a variety of roles. The lack of a coherent image of the worker has obscured the interests, power arrangement, and systems of relations through which the worker constructs the role. Closer investigation of the prison culture and its effects on the prisoner and the worker would produce key elements of a new image. The previous emphasis on the homogeneity of the guard force has been neutralized by affirmative action trends which have introduced a new set of workers to the job. At the same time, entrenched traditions which have developed out of traditional power arrangements may counter this trend. The interaction of these traditions of race and sex in the pen, and the new recruitment and hiring policies mandated by affirmative action place the role of the correctional worker in a new political and social context. As further research on the worker articulates these contextual dimensions, an understanding of the reproduction of social control will develop.

Appendix 2: Tables

Table 1
Primary Subjects—Demographics

	Ethnicity	Gender	Years in Service	Age
1	Chicano	Female	5	27
2	White	Male	6	30
3	White	Male	10	45
4	White	Female	less than 1	26
5	Chicano	Female	1	28
6	Black	Male	6-1/2	26
7	White	Male	less than 1	28
8	Chicano	Male	1	30
9	Chicano	Male	4	38
10	White	Male	9	38
11	White	Female	4	48
12	White	Male	less than 1	26
13	White	Male	9	53
14	White	Male	10	34
15	White	Male	9	31
16	White	Female	3	28
17	White	Male	20	57
18	Black	Female	5	37
19	White	Male	2	22
20	Black	Male	3	32
21	Black	Female	6	27
22	White	Male	5	27
23	White	Female	4	26
24	White	Male	4	35
25	White	Male	7	29
26	Black	Male	3	31
27	White	Male	5	30
28	Black	Female	9	40
29	Black	Male	2	27
30	Black	Male	8	43
31	Black	Female	3	31
32	White	Female	3	33
33	Black	Male	5	28
34	Chicano	Female	2	27
35	White	Female	5	33

Table 2
Prior Military Service

```
                              45%  Yes

                              55%  No
```

Table 3
Education

```
                       18%  High School

                       30%  Some College

                       48%  College Graduates
                            (BA/BS)

                        4%  Graduate School
```

Table 4
Past Law Enforcement/Corrections Experience

```
                    48%  No prior experience
                         in field

                    20%  Other CDC experience

                    17%  Police/Other Law
                         Enforcement

                    3%   Probation/Adult

                    11%  Clerical Experience**
                         (Law Enforcement and
                         Corrections)

                    ** All Female subjects
```

Table 5
Years in Service—San Quentin Correctional Officers (Interview Sample, N = 35)

Years in Service	Number of Officers	Per Cent
20	1	3%
10	2	6%
9	4	11%
8	1	3%
7	2	6%
6	2	6%
5	6	17%
4	4	11%
3	5	14%
2	3	9%
1	2	6%
less than 1	3	9%

Table 6
Years in Service—San Quentin Correctional Officers, Total Population (as of April 1982, N = 582)

Year of Hire	No. Years	Number of Officers	Per Cent	Cumulative Per Cent
1946	36	1	less than 1%	.2
1952	30	1	less than 1%	.4
1959	23	1	less than 1%	.5
1962	20	2	less than 1%	.9
1963	19	3	less than 1%	1.4
1964	18	1	less than 1%	1.6
1965	17	3	less than 1%	2.1
1966	16	8	1-1/2%	3.5
1967	15	5	less than 1%	4.4
1968	14	4	less than 1%	5.1
1969	13	5	less than 1%	6.0
1970	12	4	less than 1%	6.7
1971	11	8	1-1/2%	9.1
1972	10	6	1%	9.3
1973	9	19	3%	12.6
1974	8	19	3%	16.0
1975	7	8	1-1/2%	17.4
1976	6	9	1-1/2%	19.04
1977	5	30	5%	23.3
1978	4	39	7%	21.1
1979	3	79	14%	45.1
1980	2	65	12%	56.9
1981	1	183	33%	89.7
1982	--	58	10%	100.0
		582	100%	

Table 7
Race—Total Population, as of April 1982.

Black	33.0%
White	55.3%
Chicano	8.2%
Other	3.5%

Table 8
Race—Interview Sample, N = 35

Black	31%
White	57%
Chicano	14%

Bibliography

Alpert, Geoffrey. 1984. "The Needs of the Judiciary and the Misapplication of Social Research: The Case of Female Guards in Men's Prisons." *Criminology*, vol. 22, no. 3:441–56.

American Friends Service Committee. 1971. *Struggle for Justice*. New York: Hill and Wang.

Antilla, J. 1975. "Women in the Criminal Justice System." Helsinki, Finland: Research Institute of Legal Policy.

Attica Commission, The. 1972. *Attica: The Official Report of the New York State Commission of Attica*. New York: Praeger Publishers.

Beard, E. 1975. *Projections on the Supply of Minorities in Corrections*. Washington, D.C.: Department of Justice.

Bennett, Lawrence. 1976. "A Study of Violence in California Prisons: A Review with Policy Implications." In *Prison Violence*, ed. A. Cohen et al., pp. 149–68. Lexington, MA: Lexington Books.

Berger, Peter L., and Thomas Luckman. 1967. *The Social Construction of Reality*. New York: Anchor Books.

Blake, James. 1970. *The Joint*. Garden City, NJ: Doubleday.

Blauner, Bob. 1964. *Alienation and Freedom: The Factory Worker and His Industry*. Chicago: University of Chicago Press.

Blum, L. M. 1976. "Sources of Influence in the Socialization of Corrections Workers." Ph.D. diss., University of Michigan, Ann Arbor.

Blumer, Herbert. 1964. *Symbolic Interactionism: Perspective and Method*. Englewood Cliffs, NJ: Prentice-Hall.

Bordua, David, ed. 1967. *The Police: Six Sociological Essays*. New York: John Wiley and Sons.

Bowker, Lee H. 1980. *Prison Victimization*. New York: Elsevier.

———. 1977. *Prisoner Subcultures*. Lexington, MA: Lexington Press.

Brady, Malcolm. 1967. *On the Yard*. Boston: Little, Brown.

Brodsky, Carroll M. 1977. "Long Term Work Stress in Teachers and Prison Guards." *Journal of Occupational Medicine*, vol. 19, no. 2: 133–38.

Brodsky, S. L. 1974. "A Bill of Rights for Correctional Officers." *Federal Probation*, vol. 38, no. 2 (June): 38–40.

Brown, B. S. et al. 1971. "Staff Conceptions of Inmate Characteristics." *Criminology*, vol. 9, nos. 2, 3 (Aug.-Nov.): 316–330.

Burawoy, Michael. 1979. *Manufacturing Consent: Changes in the Labor Process Under Capitalism*. Chicago: University of Chicago Press.

Burns, H. 1969. "A Miniature Totalitarian State: Maximum Security Prison." *Canadian Journal of Criminology* 1: 153–64.

Calahan M. 1969. "Trends in Incarceration in US Since 1880." *Crime and Delinquency*, vol. 15, no. 1 (Winter): 9–41.

Carroll, Leo G. 1981. "The Frustrated Hacks." In *The Keepers: Prison Guards and Contemporary Corrections*, ed. Ben M. Crouch, pp. 302–23. Springfield, IL: Charles C. Thomas.

———. 1977. "Race and Three Forms of Prisoner Power: Confrontation, Censoriousness and Corruption." In *Contemporary Correction: Social Control and Conflict*, ed. C. R. Huff, pp. 40–53. Beverly Hills: Sage Publication.

———. 1974. *Hacks, Blacks, and Cons*. Lexington, MA: Lexington Books.

Chang, O. H., and C. H. Zastrow. 1976. "Inmates and Security Guards Perception of Themselves and Each Other." *International Journal of Criminology and Penology*, vol. 5, no. 1: 89–98.

Cheatwood, A. D. 1974. "The Staff in Correctional Settings: An Empirical Investigation of Frying Pans and Fires." *Journal of Research in Crime and Delinquency*, vol. 2, no. 2: 173–79.

Check, F. E., and M. D. Miller. 1983. "The Experience of Stress for Correctional Officers: A Double-Bind Theory of Correctional Stress." *Journal of Criminal Justice*, vol. 11, no. 2: 105–12.

———. 1982. "Reducing Staff and Inmates Stress." *Corrections Today*, vol. 44, no. 5 (October): 72–79.

Christianson, S. 1979. "Correctional Law Developments—How Unions Affect Prison Administration." *Criminal Law Bulletin*, vol. 15, no. 3 (May/June): 238–47.

Cleaver, Eldridge. 1968. *Soul on Ice*. New York: McGraw Hill.

Clemmer, Donald. 1940. *The Prison Community.* New York: Holt, Rinehart, and Winston.

Cloward, Richard, ed. 1960a. *Theoretical Studies in the Social Organization of the Prison.* New York: Social Science Research Council.

———. 1960b. "Social Control Within the Prison." In *Theoretical Studies in the Social Organization of the Prison.* New York: Social Science Research Council.

Cohen, Jay. 1979. "The Correction Academy: The Emergence of a New Institution in the Criminal Justice System." *Crime and Delinquency*, vol. 25, no. 2 (April):177–99.

Cressey, Donald. 1969. "Achievement of an Unstated Correctional Goal." In *Prisons within Society*, ed. L. Hazelrigg, pp. 50–67. Garden City, NY: Doubleday.

———. 1960. "Limitations on Organizational Treatment in Modern Prisons." In *Theoretical Studies*, ed. Richard Cloward, pp. 78–110. New York: Social Science Research Council.

———. 1959. "Contradictory Objectives in Complex Organizations: The Case of the Prison." *Administrative Science Quarterly*, vol. 4, no. 1:1–19.

Crouch, Ben M. 1982. "Sex and Occupational Socialization Among Prison Guards: A Longitudinal Study." *Criminal Justice and Behavior*, vol. 9, no. 2 (June): 159–76.

———. 1981a. "The Book vs. the Boot: Two Styles of Guarding in a Southern Prison." In *The Keepers: Prison Guards and Contemporary Correction*, ed. B. Crouch, pp. 207–24. Springfield, IL: Charles C. Thomas.

———. 1981b. "The Guard in a Changing Prison World." In *The Keepers: Prison Guards and Contemporary Corrections*, ed. B. Crouch, pp. 5–45. Springfield, IL: Charles C. Thomas.

Crouch, Ben M., and J. W. Marguart. 1981. "On Becoming a Prison Guard." In *The Keepers: Prison Guards and Contemporary Correction*, ed. B. Crouch, pp. 63–106. Springfield, IL: Charles C. Thomas.

Crouch, Ben M., and G. P. Alpert. 1980. "Prison Guards' Attitudes Towards Components of the Criminal Justice System." *Criminology*, vol. 18, no. 2 (August): 227–36.

Cullen, F. et al. 1985. "The Social Dimensions of Correctional Officer Stress." *Justice Quarterly*, vol. 2, no. 4 (December): 205–34.

Davidson, R. Ted. 1974. *Chicano Prisoners: The Key to San Quentin.* New York: Holt, Rinehart and Winston.

Doran, Robert E. 1974. "Organizational Stereotyping: The Case of the Adjustment Center Classification Committee." In *Punishment and Corrections,* ed. D. Greenberg, p. 41–68. Beverly Hills: Sage.

Downey, R. N., and E. I. Signori. 1958. "The Selection of Prison Guards." *Journal of Criminal Law, Criminology and Police Science,* vol. 49, no. 3 (Sept./Oct.): 234–36.

Duffee, David. 1979. *Correctional Policy and Prison Organization.* Beverly Hills: Sage.

————. 1974. "The Correctional Officer Subculture and Organizational Change." *Journal of Research in Crime and Delinquency,* vol. 2, no. 2 (July): 155–72.

Duffy, Clinton. 1950. *The San Quentin Story.* Garden City, NY: Doubleday.

Esselstyn, T. C. 1966. "The Social System of Correctional Workers." *Crime and Delinquency,* vol. 12, no. 2 (April): 117–24.

Etheridge, Rose et al. 1984. "Female Employees in All-Male Correctional Facilities." *Federal Probation* 28 (December): 54–65.

Fogel, David. 1979. "... *We Are the Living Proof: The Justice Model of Corrections.*" Cincinnati: Anderson.

Foote, Jennifer. 1981a. "Guard Who Complained of Bosses Forced Sex Fired." *San Francisco Examiner,* October 20, p. 8.

————. 1981b. "A Hard Look: Women Prison Guards and Sexual Harassment." *San Francisco Examiner,* October 13, p. 1.

Foucault, M. 1977. *Discipline and Punish.* New York: Pantheon Press.

Fox, James G. 1982. *Organizational and Racial Conflict in Maximum Security Prisons.* Lexington, MA: Lexington Books.

Frank, Benjamin. 1966. "The Emerging Professionalism of the C/O." *Crime and Delinquency,* vol. 12, no. 3 (July): 272–76.

Friel, Jon. 1984. "Staff Perceptions of Prisoner Life Tasks and Prisoner Perceptions of Staff Life Tasks in a Canadian Penitentiary." *Canadian Journal of Criminology,* vol. 26, no. 3: 355–57.

Galtung. E. 1961. "Prison: The Organization of Dilemma." In *The Prison: Studies in Institutional Organization and Change,* ed. D. Cressey, pp. 107–48. New York: Holt, Rinehart and Winston.

Garabedian, Peter. 1963. "Social Roles and the Process of Socialization in the Prison Community." *Social Problems,* vol. 11, no. 2 (Fall): 140–53.

Genovese, Eugene. 1972. *Roll, Jordan, Roll: The World the Slaves Made.* New York: Vantage Books.

Giallombardo, Rose. 1966. *Society of Women: A Study of a Women's Prison.* New York: John Wiley and Son.

Giddens, Anthony. 1979. *Central Problems in Social Theory: Action, Structure and Contradiction in Social Analysis.* Berkeley: University of California Press.

————.1976. *New Rules of Sociological Method: A Positive Critique of Interpretive Sociologies.* New York: Basic Books.

Gilbert, Michael J. 1980. "Developing Performance Standards for C/O's." *Corrections Today,* vol. 42, no. 3 (May/June): 1–42.

Glaser, Barney G. 1978. *Theoretical Sensitivity.* Mill Valley: The Sociology Press.

Glaser, Barney G., and Anselm Strauss. 1967. *The Discovery of Grounded Theory.* Chicago: Aldine.

Glaser, Daniel. 1964. *The Effectiveness of a Prison and Parole System.* New York: Bobbs-Merrill.

Goffman, Erving. 1961a. *Asylums: Essays in the Social Situations of Mental Patients and Other Inmates.* Garden City: Doubleday.

————. 1961b. "On the Characteristics of Total Institutions: The Inmate World." In *The Prison: Studies in Institutional Organization and Change,* ed. Donald Cressey, pp. 15–67. New York: Holt, Rinehart and Winston.

Goldstein, Barbara. 1975. "Screening for Emotional and Psychological Fitness in Correctional Officer Hiring." Washington, D.C.: American Bar Association (January).

Griswold, H. J. et al. 1970. *An Eye for an Eye.* New York: Holt, Rinehart and Winston.

Grosser, George H. 1960. "The External Setting and its Internal Relation of the Prison." In *Prisons Within Society,* ed. L. Hazelrigg, pp. 9–26. Garden City, NY: Doubleday.

Grusky, Oscar. 1959. "Role Conflict in Correctional Organization: A Study of Prison Camp Officials." *Administrative Science Quarterly* 3: 452–72.

Guenther, A. L., and M. Q. Guenther. 1974. "Screws vs. Thugs." *Society* 2 (July/Aug.): 42–50.

Haney, Craig, C. Banks, and P. Zimbardo. 1973. "Interpersonal Dynamics in a Simulated Prison." *International Journal of Criminology and Penology* 1: 69–97.

Haynor, Norman, and Elliott Ash. 1939. "The Prisoner Community as a Social Group." *American Sociological Review* 4: 262–69.

Hazelrigg, Lawrence, ed. 1969. *Prison Within Society*. Garden City, NY: Doubleday.

Heffernan, Esther. 1972. *Making It in Prison: The Square, the Cool and the Life*. New York: Wiley-Interscience.

Hepburn, J. 1987. "The Prison Control Structure and Its Effect on Work Attitudes: The Perceptions and Attitudes of Prison Guards." *Journal of Criminal Justice*, vol. 15, no. 1: 49–64.

———. 1985. "The Exercise of Power in Coercive Organizations: A Study of Prison Guards." *Criminology*, vol. 23, no. 1: 145–63.

Hepburn, J., and C. Albonetti. 1980. "Role Conflict in Correctional Institutions." *Criminology*, vol. 17, no. 4 (February): 445–57.

Howard, Clark. 1980. *American Saturday*. New York: Marek.

Howton, F. W. 1969. "Bureaucracy, Summary Punishment and the Uniform: Notes on the C.O. and His Work." *Criminologica*, vol. 7, no. 8: 59–69.

Irwin, John. 1980. *Prisons in Turmoil*. Boston: Little, Brown.

———. 1970. *The Felon*. Englewood Cliffs, NJ: Prentice-Hall.

Irwin, John, and Donald Cressey. 1962. "Thieves, Convicts and the Inmate Culture." *Social Problems*, vol. 10, no. 2: 45–155.

Jackson, George. 1979. *Soledad Brother*. New York: Coward Press.

Jacobs, James. 1985. *New Perspectives on Prisons and Imprisonment*. Ithaca, NY: Cornell University Press.

———. 1979. "The Sexual Integration of the Prison Guard Force: A Few Comments on Dothard v. Rawlinson." *University of Toledo Law Review* 10: 389–418.

———. 1978. "What Prison Guards Think." *Crime and Delinquency*, vol. 24, no. 2 (April): 185–96.

———. 1977. *Statesville: The Penitentiary in Mass Society*. Chicago: University of Chicago.

Jacobs, James, and N. Crotty. 1981. "Implication of Collective Bargaining in Prisons." In *The Keepers: Prison Guards and Contemporary Correction*, ed. B. Crouch, pp. 323–34. Springfield, IL: Charles C. Thomas.

———. 1978. *Guard Unions and the Future of Prisons*. Ithaca, New York: Cornell Univ., New York State School of Industrial and Labor Relations.

Jacobs, James, and Mary Grear. 1977. "Drop-Outs and Rejects: An Analysis of the Prison Guards Revolving Door." *Criminal Justice Review*, vol. 2, no.2: 273–90.

Jacobs, James, and Lawrence Kraft. 1978. "Integrating the Keeper: A Comparison of Black and White Guards in Illinois." *Social Problems*, vol. 25, no. 3 (February): 304–18.

Jacobs, James, and Harold Retsky. 1975. "Prison Guard." *Urban Life* 4 (April): 5–29.

Jacobs, James, and Lynn Zimmer. 1980. "A Sociological and Institutional Analysis of the 1979 N.Y. State Prison Guard Strike." Paper presented at the 1980 meetings of the American Society of Criminology Convention, October.

Johnson, Elmer. 1981. "The Changing World of the Correctional Officer." In *Prison Guard/Correctional Officer*, ed. R. Ross, pp. 777–85. Toronto: Butterworth.

Johnson, Robert, and Shelly Price. 1981. "The Complete Correctional Officer: Human Services and the Human Environment of Prison." *Criminal Justice and Behavior*,vol. 8, no. 3 (September): 343–73.

Jones, C. B. 1979. "Critical Employment Issues in County Jail." *Journal of Police Science and Administration*, vol. 7, no. 2 (June):129–37.

Jones, T. 1978. "Blacks in the American Criminal Justice System—A Study of Sanctioned Deviance." *Journal of Sociology and Social Welfare*, vol. 5, no. 3: 356–73.

Jurik, Nancy. 1985a. "An Officer and a Lady: Organizational Barriers to Women Working as Correctional Officers in Men's Prisons." *Social Problems*, vol. 32, no. 4 (April): 375–88.

———. 1985b. "Individual and Organizational Determinants of Correctional Officer Attitudes toward Inmates." *Criminology*, vol. 23, no. 3:523–39.

Jurik, Nancy, and Gregory Halemba. 1984. "Gender, Working Conditions and the Job Satisfaction of Women in a Non-Traditional Occupation: Women Correctional Officers in Men's Prisons." *Sociological Quarterly* 25 (Autumn): 551–66.

Jurik, Nancy, and Russel Winn. 1987. "Describing Correctional-Security Dropouts and Rejects: An Individual or Organizational Profile." *Criminal Justice and Behavior*, vol. 14, no. 1 (March): 5–25.

Kassebaum, G. G., O. A. Ward, and O. M. Wilmer. 1974. "Some Correlates of Staff Ideology in the Prison." *Journal of Research in Crime and Delinquency*, vol. 1, no. 2 (July): 96–107.

Katsampes, Paul. 1969. "Changing C.O.s: A Demonstration Study." *International Journal of Criminology and Penology* 4: 123–44.

Kauffman, Kelsey. 1981. "Prison Officers' Attitudes and Perceptions of Attitudes: A Case of Pluralistic Ignorance." *Journal of Research in Crime and Delinquency* 18 (July): 272–94.

King, Steven. 1982. "Rita Hayworth and the Shaw Shank Redemption." In *Different Seasons*, pp. 15–108. New York: Viking Press.

Kinsell, Lynn W., and Randall G. Sheldon. 1981. "A Survey of Correctional Officers at a Medium Security Prison." *Corrections Today*, vol. 43, no. 1: 40–51.

Kissel, P., and K. Seidel. 1980. "Women Correctional Officers in Male Institutions." Washington, D.C.: National Institute of Corrections.

Klofas, John. 1984. "Reconsidering Prison Personnel: New Views of the Correctional Officer Subculture." *International Journal of Offender Therapy and Comparative Criminology* 28: 169–75.

Klofas, John, and Hans Toch. 1982. "The Guard Subculture Myth." *Journal of Research in Crime and Delinquency*, vol. 19, no. 2 (July): 238–54.

Lamott, Kenneth. 1972. "I Didn't Bring Anyone in Here and I Can't Send Anybody Home." *Saturday Review*, vol. 55, no. 4: 8–13.

———. 1961. *Chronicles of San Quentin*. New York: David McKay.

Lombardo, Lucian X. 1981a. *Guards Imprisoned: Correctional Officers at Work*. New York: Elsevier Press.

———. 1981b. "Occupational Stress in Correctional Officers: Sources, Coping Strategies and Implications." In *Corrections at the Crossroads*, ed. S. Zimmerman and H. Miller, pp. 129–49. Beverly Hills: Sage.

Lunden, Walter. 1965. *The Prison Warden and the Custodial Staff*. Springfield, IL: Charles C. Thomas.

Manning, Will. 1983. "An Underlying Cause of Burn-Out." *Corrections Today*, vol. 45, no. 1 (February): 20–22.

Manocchio, Anthony, and Jimmy Dunn. 1970. *The Time Game: Two Views of the Prison*. Beverly Hills: Sage Publication.

Marquart, J., and B. Crouch. 1985. "Judicial Reform and Prisoner Control: The Impact of Ruiz v. Estelle on a Texas Penitentiary." *Law and Society Review* 19: 557–87.

Marquart, J., and Juliana Roebuck. 1986. "Prison Guards and Snitches: Social Control in a Maximum Security Institution." In *The Dilemma of Punishment*, ed. K. Haas and G. Alpert, pp. 158–76. Prospect Heights: Waveland Press.

Martin, George N. 1980. "Stress and the Warden." *Corrections Today*, vol. 42, no. 6 (Nov./Dec).

Martin, Joanne. 1983. "Organizational Culture and Counterculture." Working Papers. Stanford, CA: School of Business, Stanford University.

Martin, Roger. 1980. *Pigs and Other Animals*. Arcadia Press: Myco.

Marx, Karl. 1972. "Estranged Labor." In *The Marx and Engels Reader*, ed. R. C. Tucker. New York: W. W. Norton.

May, Edgar. 1976. "Prison Guards in America—The Inside Story." *Corrections Magazine*, vol. 2, no. 6: 4–5.

McCleery, Richard. 1960. "Communications Patterns as Bases of Systems of Authority." In *Theoretical Studies*, ed. Richard Cloward, pp. 49–77. New York: Social Science Research Council.

McCorkle, L., and R. Korn. 1954. "Resocialization Within Walls." *The Annals of the American Academy of Political and Social Sciences* 23 (May): 88–90.

McCoy, John. 1981. *Concrete Mama: Prison Profiles from Walla Walla*. Columbia: University of Missouri Press.

McKee, Richard. 1981. *Prisons and Politics*. Lexington, MA: Lexington Books.

McWarton, William C. 1981. *Inmate Society: Legs, Half-pants and Gunmen: A Study of Inmate Guards*. Saratoga, CA: Century 21 Publishing.

Mead, George Herbert. 1964 [1956]. *George Herbert Mead on Social Psychology*, ed. A. Strauss. Chicago: University of Chicago Press.

Melossi, Dario. 1985. "Overcoming the Crisis in Criminology." *Criminology*, vol. 23, no. 2 (May): 193–200.

Mills, C. Wright. 1940. "Situated Actions and Vocabularies of Motives." *American Sociological Review* (December):904–13.

Mitford, Jessica. 1971. *Kind and Usual Punishment*. New York: Alfred A. Knopf.

Montilla, M. 1978. *Prison Employee Unionism: A Guide for Correctional Administration*. Washington, D.C.: National Institute of Justice.

Moore, Joan. 1978. *Homeboys*. Philadelphia: Temple University Press.

Moos, Randolph. 1968. "The Assessment of Social Climates of Correctional Institutions." *Journal of Research in Crime and Delinquency*, vol. 5, no. 2 (July):178–88.

Morris, Pauline. 1963. "Staff Problems in a Maximum Security Prison." *Prison Services Journal*, vol. 2, no. 6: 32–43.

Morris, T., and P. Morris. 1963. *Pentonville: A Sociological Study of an English Prison*. London: Routledge and Kegan Paul.

Muir, William. 1977. *The Police: Street Corner Politicians*. Chicago: University of Chicago Press.

Murton, Thomas. 1969. *Accomplices to the Crime*. New York: Grove Press.

National Bar Association. 1978. "Minority Involvement in the Criminal Justice System—Report of Findings." Washington, D.C.: Department of Justice.

National Council on Crime and Delinquency. 1976. "Women in Criminal Justice—A Policy Statement." *Crime and Delinquency*, vol. 22, no. 1 (January):1–2.

Newsweek. 1971. "Attica Manifesto/Demands," Sept. 27, p. 32.

O'Leary, V., D. Duffee, and E. Werk. 1977. "Developing Relevant Data for a Prison Organization Development Program." *Journal of Criminal Justice*, vol. 5, no. 2 (Summer): 85–103.

O'Neal, Carl F. 1965. "Professional and Custody Staff Must Merge Their Treatment Efforts." *Federal Probation*, vol. 29, no. 3 (September): 45–50.

Owen, Barbara A. 1985. "Race and Gender Relations among Prison Workers." *Crime and Delinquency*, vol. 31, no. 1 (January):147–59.

Parisi, Nicolette. 1984. "The Female Correctional Officer: Her Progress toward and Prospects for Equality." *The Prison Journal*, vol. 64, no. 1 (Spring/Summer): 92–109.

Park, Robert. 1976. "The Organization of Prison Violence." In *Prison Violence*, ed. A. Cohen et al., pp. 79–88. Lexington, MA: Lexington Books.

Peretti, Peter, and Margaret Hooker. 1976. "Social Role Self-Perceptions of State Prison Guards." *Criminal Justice and Behavior*, vol. 3, no. 2 (June): 187–95.

Peterson, Cheryl B. 1982. "Doing Time with the Boys: An Analysis of Women Correctional Officers in All-Male Facilities." In *The Criminal Justice System and Women*, ed. B. Price and N. Sokoloff. New York: Clark Boardman.

Philliber, Susan. 1987. "Thy Brother's Keeper: A Review of the Literature on Correctional Officers." *Justice Quarterly*, vol. 4, no. 1 (March): 9–37.

Pogrebin, Mark. 1978. "Role Conflict Among Correctional Officers in Treatment Oriented Correctional Institutions." *International Journal of Offender Therapy and Comparative Criminology*, vol. 22, no. 2: 242–259.

———. 1977. "Administrative Demands on Impediments to Treatment in Correctional Institutions." *Reform in Corrections: Problems and Issues*, ed. H. Allen and N. Beran, pp. 107–16. New York: Praeger Publishers.

Poole, E. D., and R. M. Regoli. 1981. "Alienation among Prison Guards: An Examination of the Work Relations of Prison Guards." *Criminology*, vol. 19, no. 2: 251–70.

———. 1980a. "Role Stress, Custody Orientation and Disciplinary Acts." *Criminology*, vol. 18, no. 2 (August): 215–26.

———. 1980b. "Examining the Impact of Professionalism on Cynicism, Role Conflict and Work Alienation among Prison Guards." *Criminal Justice Review*, vol. 5, no. 2: 57–65.

Porter, Bruce. 1982. "California Prison Gangs: The Price of Control." *Corrections Magazine*, vol. 8, no. 6 (December):6–21.

Potter, J. 1979. "Guard Unions—The Search for Solidarity." *Corrections Magazine*, vol. 5, no. 3 (September): 25–35.

Prigmore, C. S., and J. C. Watkins. 1972. "Correctional Manpower: Are We the Society of Captives?" *Federal Probation*, vol. 36, no. 4 (December): 12–17.

Ross, Robert R. 1981. "Is a C/O by Any Other Name, a 'Screw?' " In *Prison Guard/Correctional Officer: The Use and Abuse of the Human Resources of the Prison*, ed. R. Johnson, pp. 87–104. Toronto: Butterworth.

Rothman, David. 1971. *The Discovery of the Asylum*. Boston: Little, Brown.

Roucek, Joseph. 1935. "Sociology of the Prison Guards." *Sociology and Social Research*, vol. 20, no. 2 (Nov./Dec.): 143–51.

Rudoff, A. 1960. "Prison Inmates: An Involuntary Association." Ph.D. diss. Department of Sociology, University of California, Berkeley.

Rusche, Otto, and Georg Kirchheimer. 1939. *Punishment and Social Structure*. New York: Columbia University Press.

Schragg, Clarence. 1944. "Social Types in a Prison Community." Master's thesis, Washington State University.

Schroeder, A. 1976. *Shaking It Rough*. Garden City, NY: Doubleday.

Schutz, Alfred. 1976 [1967]. *The Phenomenology of the Social World*. London: Heinemann Educational Books.

Scudder, Kenyon F. 1952. *Prisoners Are People*. Garden City, NY: Doubleday.

Shamir, Boaz, and Amos Drory. 1981a. "Occupational Tedium among Prison Officers." *Criminal Justice and Behavior*, vol. 9, no. 1: 79–99.

———. 1981b. "Some Correlates of Prison Guards' Beliefs." *Criminal Justice and Behavior*, vol. 8, no. 2: 233–49.

Skolnick, Jerome. 1962. *Justice Without Trial*. New York: John Wiley and Sons.

Smith, Carol, and John Hepburn. 1979. "Alienation in Prison Organizations." *Criminology*, vol. 17, no. 2 (August): 251–62.

Smith-Merrow, L. W. 1962. *Prison Screw*. London: Herbert Jenkins.

Sobell, Martin. 1974. *On Doing Time*. New York: Bantam Books.

Stastny, C., and G. Tyrnauer. 1982. *Who Rules the Joint?: The Changing Political Culture of Maximum Security Prisons in America*. Lexington, MA: Lexington Books.

Staudohar, Paul D. 1976. "Prison Guard Labor Relations in Ohio." *Industrial Relations*, vol. 15, no. 2 (May): 177–90.

Stinchcomb, Jeanne. 1986. "Correctional Officer Stress: Looking at the Causes, You May Be the Cure." Paper presented at the Academy of Criminal Justice Sciences, Orlando, Florida, April.

Stotland, Ezra. 1976. "Self Esteem and Violence by Guards and State Troopers at Attica." *Criminal Justice and Behavior*, vol. 3, no. 1 (March): 85–95.

Street, David. 1965. "The Inmate Group in Custodial and Treatment Settings." *American Sociological Review*, (February): 40–55.

Stutsman, Jesse O. 1936. "The Prison Staff." *The Annals* 157 (September): 62–71.

Sudnow, David. 1965. "Normal Crimes: Sociological Features of the Penal Code in a Public Defender's Office." *Social Problems*, vol. 12, no. 2 (Winter): 225–64.

Sullivan, T. T. 1977. "Importance Given Selected Job Characteristics by Individuals Who Possess a Criminal Justice Degree." *Criminal Justice Review*, vol. 4, no. 2 (Fall): 93–100.

Sulty, Thomas A. 1980. *Correctional Officer Training Manuals*. Washington, D.C.: National Institute of Corrections.

Suttles, Gerald. 1968. *The Social Order of the Slum.* Chicago: University of Chicago Press.

Sykes, Gresham. 1958. *Society of Captives.* Princeton, NJ: Princeton University Press.

————. 1956. "Men, Merchants and Toughs." *Social Problems* 4 (October): 130–83.

Sykes, Gresham, and Sheldon Messinger. 1960. "The Inmate Social System." In *Theoretical Studies,* ed. Richard Cloward, pp. 5–19. New York: Social Science Research System.

Tagaki, Paul. 1975. "The Walnut Street Jail: A Penal Reform to Centralize the State." *Federal Probation,* vol. 39, no. 4: 18–25.

Tasker, Robert J. 1927. *Grimhaven.* New York: Alfred A. Knopf.

Terkle, Studs. 1972. *Working.* New York: Avon Books.

Thacker, Jo Anne. 1979. "Reducing Burn-Out." *Corrections Today,* vol. 41, no. 6 (Nov./Dec.):50–51.

Thomas, C. W., and D. M. Petersen. 1977. *Prison Organization/Inmate Subcultures.* New York: Bobbs-Merrill.

Thomas, James E. 1972. *The English Prison Officer Since 1850.* London: Routledge and Kegan Paul.

Thompson, E. P. 1963. *The Making of the English Working Class.* New York: Random House.

Toch, Hans. 1977. "Police, Prisons and the Problem of Violence." Washington, D.C.: U.S. Government Printing Office.

Toch, Hans, and J. Douglas Grant. 1983. *Grass Roots Management: Worker Participation in Assembly Lines and Staff Participation in Client Assembly Lines.* Beverly Hills: Sage.

Toch, Hans, and John Klofas. 1982. "Alienation and Desire for Job Enrichment Among C.O.'s." *Federal Probation,* vol. 46, no. 2.

Touraine, Alain. 1977. *The Self-Production of Society.* Chicago: University of Chicago Press.

Turner, Ralph H. 1976. "The Real Self: From Institution to Impulse." *American Journal of Sociology,* vol. 81, no.5: 989–1,016.

University Research Corporation. 1979. "Management of Stress Corrections." Washington, D.C.: National Institution of Justice.

Voight, L. L. 1949. *History of California State Correctional Administrations from 1930–1940.* San Francisco: n.p.

Wahler, Cindy, and Paul Gendreau. 1985. "Assessing Correctional Officers." *Federal Probation,* vol. 69, no. 1: 70–74.

Wallace, Robert. 1966. "Ecological Implications of a Custody Institution." *Issues in Criminology*, vol. 2, no. 1 (47–60).

Wambaugh, Joseph. 1972. *The Blue Knight*. Boston: Little, Brown.

Ward, David. 1960. *Prison Rule Enforcements and Changing Organizational Goals*. Urbana: University of Illinois.

Ward, David, and Gene Kessebaum. 1965. *Women's Prison*. Chicago: Aldine.

Ward, Linda H. 1981. "Corrections Officers, Today." *Corrections Today*, vol. 43, no. 1 (Jan./Feb.): 5–12.

Ward, R. J., and D. Vangergoot. 1977. "Corrections Officers with Caseloads." *Offender Rehabilitation*, vol. 2, no. 1 (Fall): 31–38.

Webb, G. L., and D. Morris. 1978. *Prison Guards: The Culture and Perspective of an Occupational Group*. Austin: Coker Books.

Weinberg, S. K. 1941–42. "Aspects of the Prison Social Structure." *American Journal of Sociology* 47: 717–26.

Wicker, Tom. 1975. *A Time to Die*. New York: Quadrangle Press.

Wicks, R. J. 1980. *Guard! Society's Professional Prisoner*. Houston, TX: Gulf Publications.

———. 1974. "Is the C.O. a Second Class Citizen?" *American Journal of Corrections*, vol. 36, no. 1: 32–36.

Wilensky, Harold. 1964. "The Professionalization of Everyone?" *American Journal of Sociology*, vol. 70, no. 2 (September): 137–38.

Williams, Virgil, and Mary Fish. 1974. *Convicts, Codes and Contraband*. Cambridge: Balinger.

Willis, Paul, 1977. *Learning to Labour*. London: Saxon House.

Willit, T. C. 1983. "Prison Guards in Private." *Canadian Journal of Criminology*, vol. 25, no. 1: 1–17.

Wilson, Wayne. 1981. "A Prison System at Bay—The Turmoil Within." *Sacramento Bee*, Nov.

Wright, Erik Olin. 1973. *The Politics of Punishment*. New York: Harper and Row.

Wynne, John M., Jr. 1978. "Prison Employee Unionism: The Impact on Correctional Administration and Programs." Washington, D.C.: Department of Justice.

Yaley, Barbara, and Tony Platt. 1982. *Prisoner Labor: The Political Economy of California and California Prisons: 1849–1949* (unpublished manuscript). University of California, Berkeley.

Yee, Min S. 1973. *The Melancholy History of Soledad Prison*. New York: Harpers Magazine Press.

Zald, Meyer. 1962. "Power Balance and Staff Conflict in Correctional Institutions." *Administrative Science Quarterly* 17 (June): 22–29.

Zimmer, Lynn E. 1986. *Women Guarding Men.* Chicago: University of Chicago Press.

Index

About the Author

BARBARA A. OWEN received a Ph.D. in Sociology from the University of California, Berkeley in 1984. As a postdoctoral fellow with the Alcohol Research Group, Dr. Owen then conducted a comparative study of drug and alcohol patterns among parolees. She has taught sociology and criminology at Eastern Washington University and on several campuses of the University of California.

Currently, Barbara Owen is a Research Analyst with the Federal Bureau of Prisons where she continues her work on prison issues.